Contents

How to use this book

This book provides three sets of exam papers that mirror the AQA GCSE exam papers.

The audio, teacher-examiner parts (for Paper 2: Speaking), model answers and mark schemes can be accessed using the QR codes throughout the book or by visiting http://www.oxfordsecondary.co.uk/aqagcse-spanish-pp.

The exam papers contain hints and tips. The first set of papers provides tips for all questions and all skills, in order to help you gain confidence in answering questions. In the second set of papers there are fewer tips for listening and reading. The third set of papers does not contain tips, so that you have an opportunity to practise answering questions independently in an exam situation.

AQA GCSE Spanish Higher

AQA GCSE Spanish is made up of four exam papers, each with a weighting of 25% towards the final mark. The Higher Tier is for students targeting Grades 4–9. For more details about the specification and for the most up-to-date assessment information, please see the AQA website.

Paper 1: Listening

There are 45 minutes to complete the listening paper and 50 marks available. In Section A, the questions are in English and the answers required will either be non-verbal or in English. In Section B, the questions are in Spanish and the answers required will either be non-verbal or in Spanish.

The time includes 5 minutes at the start of the exam to read through the paper. Practise reading through the paper in this time. You may need to skim-read to get all the way through it, but try to use the time in a focused way. Identify the questions where you need to give several answers about the audio passage, or more than one piece of information, so that you're ready to listen out for the details you need. It's also good to read Section B carefully to make sure you understand the questions being asked.

The level of difficulty varies throughout the paper so don't lose heart if you encounter a hard question early on, as it doesn't mean you will find the questions that follow even harder. In AQA GCSE Paper 1, there are some questions that appear both on the Foundation and Higher Tier papers.

Use the tips in the Set 1 and Set 2 listening papers in this book to build your confidence in exam technique and to help you listen out for the correct answers.

Paper 2: Speaking

There are 60 marks available for the speaking paper. For Higher Tier, you will have supervised preparation time of 12 minutes followed by an exam of 10–12 minutes.

There are three parts to the exam:

- Role-play (15 marks) – this will last approximately 3 minutes for Higher Tier
- Photo card (15 marks) – this will last approximately 2 minutes for Higher Tier
- General Conversation (30 marks) – this will last between 5–7 minutes for Higher Tier

The candidate chooses one theme for the general conversation and the other theme will be the one that hasn't been covered in the photo card. Here is a chart showing the possible test sequences based on the candidate's choice of theme:

Role-play	Candidate's chosen conversation theme	Photo card	Candidate's second conversation theme
1, 2 or 3	Theme 1: Identity and culture	B	Theme 3
		C	Theme 2
	Theme 2: Local, national, international and global areas of interest	A	Theme 3
		C	Theme 1
	Theme 3: Current and future study and employment	A	Theme 2
		B	Theme 1

Each paper in this book contains a role-play and a photo card from each theme. The teacher-examiner part and two marked sample responses for each can be found online. For general conversation, there are two marked sample responses included in the book for each paper, followed by tasks to complete, with the following combinations of themes:

- Set 1 covers Themes 1 and 2
- Set 2 covers Themes 2 and 3
- Set 3 covers Themes 3 and 1

Tips are provided for the role-plays and photo cards in the Set 1 and Set 2 speaking papers in this book to help you respond more fully to the questions asked and anticipate the unexpected questions.

Paper 3: Reading

There is 1 hour to complete the reading paper, with 60 marks available. In Section A, the questions are in English and the answers required will either be non-verbal or in English. In Section B, the questions are in Spanish and the answers required will either be non-verbal or in Spanish. Different types of written texts are used in the reading paper, including literary extracts. In this book, example answers are given if further guidance is needed on how to answer a question, so watch out for these.

The level of difficulty varies throughout the paper so don't lose heart if you encounter a hard question early on as it doesn't mean you will find the questions that follow even harder. In AQA GCSE Paper 3, there are some questions that appear both on the Foundation and Higher Tier papers.

In Section C, there is a translation from Spanish into English with a minimum of 50 words.

Use the tips in the Set 1 and Set 2 reading papers in this book to build your confidence in exam technique and to help you pick out the correct answers from the text.

Paper 4: Writing

There is 1 hour 15 minutes to complete the writing paper and there are 60 marks available. All answers should be written in Spanish.

For Higher Tier there are three questions:

- Question 1 (16 marks): One of a choice of two structured writing tasks of 90 words, with a series of bullet points to cover in your response. In AQA GCSE Paper 4, this question is the same as question 4 on the Foundation Tier paper.

- Question 2 (32 marks): One of a choice of two writing tasks of 150 words, with a series of bullet points to cover in your response.

- Question 3 (12 marks): A translation from English into Spanish of a minimum of 50 words.

For Question 1, check whether you are required to use the familiar or polite 'you' form in your answer. In AQA GCSE Paper 4, this can vary from year to year, so you must read the instructions carefully.

Tips are provided in the Set 1 and Set 2 writing papers in this book, to help you respond to the questions and to give guidance on extending your answers. Two marked model answers are included online for questions 1 and 2. Also included online is a mark scheme for question 3.

AQA GCSE Spanish (9–1)

H

Higher Tier Paper 1 Listening

Time allowed: 45 minutes
(including 5 minutes' reading time before the test)

You will need no other materials.
The pauses are pre-recorded for this test.

Information

- The marks for the questions are shown in brackets. The maximum mark for this paper is 50.
- You must **not** use a dictionary.

Advice

This is what you should do for each item.

- After the question number is announced, there will be a pause to allow you to read the instructions and questions.
- Listen carefully to the recording and read the questions again.
- Listen to the recording again, and then answer the questions.
- When the next question is about to start you will hear a bleep.
- You may write at any time during the test.
- In **Section A**, answer the questions in **English**. In **Section B**, answer the questions in **Spanish**.
- You must answer all the questions in the spaces provided. Do not write on blank pages.
- Write neatly and put down all the information you are asked to give.
- **You must not ask questions or interrupt during the test.**
- You have five minutes to read through the question paper. You may make notes during this time. You may turn to the questions now.
- **The test starts now.**

Listen to the audio

Please note: The Practice Paper questions and answers have not been written or approved by AQA.

Section A   Questions and answers in **English**

News headlines

You are listening to the following news items on a Mexican radio station.

A	Youth unemployment rises
B	Presidential elections take place
C	Pupils restore local bridge
D	Large donation sends message of support to migrants
E	Peaceful protest against foreign leader
F	Youths march against climate change
G	Recent extreme weather conditions finally set to end

Match the headline to each item of news.

Write the correct letter in each box.

- Be prepared to listen out for synonyms (different words that have the same or similar meanings). It is unlikely that the key words in the statements A–G will be the same as those you hear.
- Make a note of the Spanish words that are associated with some of these headings which you can listen out for. For example, 'bridge' is *el puente*, 'unemployment/to be unemployed' is *el paro/estar en paro*. Likewise, there may be an amount of money mentioned for the news item about a large donation (i.e. 3 million Euros).

0 1   **[1 mark]**

0 2   **[1 mark]**

0 3   **[1 mark]**

0 4   **[1 mark]**

0 5   **[1 mark]**

Protecting the environment

You are listening online to a radio programme. Some Cuban activists are explaining what they do to protect the environment.

Complete the information they give.

Answer in **English**.

> - For this type of question, precision and detail are key. Only include relevant detail in your answers as you can lose marks by adding incorrect information.
> - It is often not enough to recognise and write down one key word that you have understood! For example, in question 7, if you hear 'peces del río local', make sure you write 'fish from the local river'; you will not be awarded the mark if you simply write 'fish' on its own.

Example   This week they have protected **abandoned dogs** to support **animal rights**.

0 6   Next week they will protect _____ to support

_____

[2 marks]

0 7   Last week they protected _____ to support

_____

[2 marks]

0 8   **Conflict at work**

You are watching a TV programme in Spanish. Marcelo, the main character, is arguing with his boss, Cristina.

Answer **both** parts of the question in **English**.

> - If you're asked to give a reason, the audio will usually include the word *porque*.
> - Listen out for the little negative words like *no, nunca, nada, nadie* as these are likely to be heard when someone is expressing negative opinions.
> - Always answer every question and if you're really stuck, think of cognates.

0 8 . 1   Why has Marcelo not been happy in his job lately? Give **two** reasons.

_____

_____

[2 marks]

0 8 . 2   What is Cristina's solution?

_____

[1 mark]

Around town

You hear a conversation between your best friend, Ánima, and her mother.

Answer in **English**.

> - Read the question carefully to make sure your answers provide the right level of detail. A partial answer, or one that is too vague, will not gain the mark.
> - Always listen carefully to the second playing of the recording. In question 9, for example, you may hear that Ánima wants her mother to give her a lift on the first playing, but pick up the extra detail that she specifically wants a lift with her friends to the cinema during the second playing.

0 9   What would Ánima like her mother to do?

_____

[1 mark]

1 0   What would she like her father to do?

_____

[1 mark]

   AQA GCSE Spanish Higher Practice Papers © Oxford University Press 2020. Photocopying prohibited

1 1   **Interview with a Spanish nutritionist**

You are listening to an interview about eating habits with nutritionist Salvador Mallo.

Answer **all** parts of the question in **English**.

> • When you hear an interview, listen to the interviewer carefully – their questions are likely to follow the order of the questions in the paper. Use the time to focus and prepare yourself for the answer material that follows.
> • Remember that you don't have to write full sentences in English, as long as you include all the necessary details.
> • There are clues in the questions that might help you locate the answers in the recording. For example, in 11.3, listen out for the words *joven/jóvenes* ('young person'/'young people'), *se debe/deben* ('one must/they must'), and/or *nunca* or *jámas* ('never').

1 1 . 1   According to Salvador, what is it becoming harder for young people to do nowadays?

_____

[1 mark]

1 1 . 2   Why does Salvador think it is a good idea to avoid buying fatty and sugary foods in the supermarket?

_____

[1 mark]

1 1 . 3   According to Salvador, young people must never…

A	use salt when cooking.
B	go on a diet without consulting a doctor.
C	eat more than five portions of fruit and vegetables per day.

Write the correct letter in the box.   [ ]   **[1 mark]**

Answer the question in **English**.

1 2   How do we know Salvador is a fan of home cooking? Mention **two** reasons.

_____

_____

[2 marks]

School life

You are listening to a Spanish radio phone-in where student callers are describing how teachers have helped them.

> - Use your 5 minutes' reading time at the start of the exam to read the questions carefully and make notes.
> - From the multiple-choice answers, try to predict what kinds of words you might hear. For example, in 13, listen carefully for 'Christmas' (*las Navidades*); 'homework' (*los deberes*) or 'private' (*privado*) and eliminate the least likely answer(s) as soon as possible.
> - This type of question often benefits most from a careful second listening.

1 3 Casilda's teachers…

A	offered her specific advice before Christmas.
B	gave her more homework when she failed her exams.
C	decided to arrange private tutoring for her.

Write the correct letter in the box. **[1 mark]**

1 4 Samuel's teachers…

A	quickly organised a transfer to a new school.
B	supported him when he was falsely accused of insulting a student.
C	spoke to the parents of a student who was bullying him.

Write the correct letter in the box. **[1 mark]**

1 5 Aitana's teachers…

A	made sure she didn't go hungry.
B	gave her extra lessons for three months.
C	got her mum a job in the school canteen.

Write the correct letter in the box. **[1 mark]**

La Feria de Abril

You are watching a Spanish TV programme in which the organiser of the annual Seville Fair is being interviewed.

What questions does the interviewer ask her?

Answer in **English**.

Example   <u>Can you bring dogs to the Fair?</u>

> • Always read the question title as this will help you to understand the context of what you are about to hear. Here, for example, an interviewer is talking to the organiser of the annual Seville fair, so the questions must revolve around the organisational aspects of her work.
> • Practise question words carefully prior to your exam and make sure you include as much detail as possible. Partial answers are unlikely to gain a mark.

1 6

_____

_____

[1 mark]

1 7

_____

_____

[1 mark]

1 8

_____

_____

[1 mark]

1 9

_____

_____

[1 mark]

Talking about jobs and careers

You are talking to two young professionals, Esteban and Lucrecia, about the different jobs they have had.

Which jobs did they like?

Which jobs have they never done?

A	Travel agent
B	Ticket seller
C	Firefighter
D	Chef
E	Farmer
F	Bus driver
G	Tour guide
H	Interpreter
I	Actor
J	Bricklayer
K	Nurse

- There are many marks available for this type of question, and a lot of detail to listen to, so try to maintain a high level of concentration and take brief notes as you listen.
- The questions offer clues to help you: you would expect to hear positive opinions to describe jobs that the speaker likes, for example, and to hear *nunca* or *jamás* for jobs the speaker has never tried.
- Think about Spanish words that are associated with the professions, such as *viajar*, *guía turístico* (travel agent); *la cocina*, *cocinar* (chef); *hospital*, *enfermero* (nurse).

Write the correct letter in each box.

Answer **both** parts of the question.

2 0 . 1 Esteban liked being a… [2 marks]

2 0 . 2 Esteban has never been a… [2 marks]

Answer **both** parts of the question.

2 1 . 1 Lucrecia liked being a… [2 marks]

2 1 . 2 Lucrecia has never been a… [2 marks]

| 2 | 2 | **Mobile phones**

You are listening to a Spanish radio programme discussing the use of mobile phones.

What two issues will the programme be looking into?

Complete the phrases in **English**.

- In this type of question, listen out for the relevant Spanish vocabulary that signals the start of the key details required to answer correctly. For example, in 22.1, you are listening out for *Las aplicaciones que…* and in 22.2, *El número de…* .
- Longer answers are usually indicated by two lines provided for the written answer, so you are expected to provide all the details you hear.

| 2 | 2 |.| 1 | Apps that…

_____

_____

| 2 | 2 |.| 2 | The number of…

_____

_____

[2 marks]

Once again, beware of distractors. You are likely to hear all of the vocabulary appearing in a multiple-choice question, but in this question, only one option conveys what the expert recommends. Listen out for language such as *en mi opinión* ('in my opinion'); *recomiendo* ('I recommend'), *aconsejo* ('I advise') etc.

| 2 | 3 | What does the expert recommend?

A	Not using a phone before going to sleep.
B	Avoiding social media use in the evening.
C	A stress-free lifestyle.

Write the correct letter in the box.

[1 mark]

| 2 | 4 | | **Social issues** |

You are watching a Spanish television debate in which people are discussing social issues that concern them.

For each speaker, choose their area of concern.

Write the correct letter in each box.

A	Health care
B	Youth unemployment rate
C	Knife crime
D	The housing market
E	Family conflict

> - It is unlikely that the key words in the statements A–E will be the same as those you hear in the audio. Think of Spanish words associated with some of these headings which you can listen out for: for example, 'health' (*la salud*), 'unemployment' (*el paro*), 'jobs' (*los empleos*), 'housing' (*la vivienda*), 'knife' (*el cuchillo*).
> - You will probably hear words that seem to refer to many possible answers. Try to get a feeling for the topic being discussed and to avoid being thrown off course by single words.

Answer **all** parts of the question.

| 2 | 4 | . | 1 | Diana | [1 mark]

| 2 | 4 | . | 2 | Gerardo | [1 mark]

| 2 | 4 | . | 3 | Pamela | [1 mark]

Section B   Questions and answers in **Spanish**

Las actividades de tiempo libre

Estás escuchando un programa de radio. Dos chicos hablan de su tiempo libre.

¿De qué actividades hablan?

Escribe la letra correcta en cada casilla.

A	el automovilismo
B	el ciclismo
C	el judo
D	el tenis
E	el piragüismo
F	el bádminton
G	el atletismo
H	la natación

- There is a lot of information to digest, so try to maintain your concentration and take notes.
- Listen out for time markers, for example, Past: *cuando tenía siete años*; Present: *actualmente*; Future: *el año que viene*, as these will help you identify which tense is being used.

2 5   De pequeña Susa prefería ⬚, ahora prefiere ⬚.   **[2 marks]**

2 6   De pequeño Roberto prefería ⬚, pronto hará ⬚.   **[2 marks]**

Las relaciones personales

¿Qué le preocupa a Leonor de cada miembro de su familia?

Completa las frases en **español**.

In Section B, read the instructions carefully and pay close attention to any examples, so that you know how to answer. In this case, the infinitive form of the verb is required for each answer. Realising this makes the task much easier!

Ejemplo   Con su padre, prefiere no **hablar** ni **discutir** sobre el instituto.

2 7   A causa de su madre, Leonor no puede _____ ni _____ hasta muy tarde.

[2 marks]

2 8   Su hermana no quiere _____ ni _____ su ropa con ella.

[2 marks]

Opiniones sobre el divorcio

Tus amigos argentinos, Camila y Alberto, hablan del divorcio de sus padres.

¿Qué opiniones expresan sobre el divorcio?

Escribe

P si la opinión es **positiva**.

N si la opinión es **negativa**.

P+N si la opinión es **positiva** y **negativa**.

> - Look for adjectives and verbs which express a positive or negative opinion: for example, *la vida* (life) is *mucho mejor* (much better) or *el divorcio* (divorce) is *imprescindible* (essential).
> - It helps to listen out for conjunctions of contrast such as *sin embargo, no obstante, mientras que, en cambio* etc.

| 2 9 | |

[1 mark]

| 3 0 | |

[1 mark]

END OF QUESTIONS

Answers and mark schemes

AQA GCSE Spanish (9–1)

PRACTICE PAPER

H

Higher Tier Paper 2 Speaking

Time allowed: 10–12 minutes
(+12 minutes' supervised preparation time)

Candidate's material – Role-play and Photo card

Instructions

- During the preparation time you must prepare the Role-play card and Photo card given to you.
- You may make notes during the preparation time on the paper provided by your teacher-examiner. Do not write on the stimulus cards.
- Hand your notes and both stimulus cards to the teacher-examiner before the General Conversation.
- You must ask the teacher-examiner at least one question in the General Conversation.

Information

- The test will last a maximum of 12 minutes and will consist of a Role-play (approximately 2 minutes) and a Photo card (approximately 3 minutes), followed by a General Conversation (between 5 and 7 minutes) based on your nominated Theme and the remaining Theme which has not been covered in the Photo card.
- You must **not** use a dictionary at any time during the test. This includes the preparation time.

Teacher Part

Please note: The Practice Paper questions and answers have not been written or approved by AQA.

ROLE-PLAY 1

CANDIDATE'S ROLE

Part 1

Instructions to candidates

Your teacher will play the part of a ticket office assistant in the Valencia football stadium and will speak first.

You should address the assistant as *usted*.

When you see this – **!** – you will have to respond to something you have not prepared.

When you see this – **?** – you will have to ask a question.

Estás hablando con un empleado / una empleada del estadio de fútbol de Valencia.

- Entradas – número

- **?** Partido – fecha

- **!**

- Tu opinión sobre el fútbol español y una razón

- Tus otros planes en Valencia (**dos** detalles)

- For the role-play section of your speaking exam, the most important thing is getting the message across clearly, so keep your responses as simple and clear as possible.
- Each response should contain a verb used in the correct form and just enough relevant detail to fulfil the task.
- When two details are required, it does not mean that two verb forms are needed. So, for bullet 5 in this task for example, two marks could be achieved if you say something like *voy a ir al parque* (first detail) *con mis hermanos mayores* (second detail).

ROLE-PLAY 2

CANDIDATE'S ROLE

Part 1

Instructions to candidates

Your teacher will play the part of your Argentinian friend and will speak first.

You should address your friend as *tú*.

When you see this – **!** – you will have to respond to something you have not prepared.

When you see this – **?** – you will have to ask a question.

> Estás hablando con tu amigo argentino / tu amiga argentina sobre el instituto.
>
> • Tu opinión sobre las asignaturas
>
> • Las instalaciones – **una** ventaja
>
> • **!**
>
> • Comida en la cantina ayer (**dos** detalles)
>
> • **?** El uniforme escolar en Argentina

> • When preparing each bullet point in the role-play, make sure any verb you use is in the correct tense (past, present or future) and person ('I', 'you', 'we' etc.). In bullet 4, for example, note that the word *ayer* (yesterday) appears on the candidate's role, which means that past tenses are required.
> • It is common for students to repeat the teacher-examiner's question and mistakenly respond in the *tú* ('you') form, rather than the *yo* ('I') form. For example, in bullet 4, if the teacher-examiner asks ¿*Qué* **comiste** *en la cantina ayer?* ('What **did you eat** in the canteen yesterday?'), you need to reply using the *yo* ('I') form **comí** ('I ate…').

ROLE-PLAY 3

CANDIDATE'S ROLE

Part 1

Instructions to candidates

Your teacher will play the part of your Chilean friend and will speak first.

You should address your friend as *tú*.

When you see this – **!** – you will have to respond to something you have not prepared.

When you see this – **?** – you will have to ask a question.

Estás hablando con tu amigo chileno / tu amiga chilena sobre llevar una vida sana.

- Tu dieta – lo bueno y lo malo (**dos** detalles)

- Qué hiciste para estar en forma la semana pasada (**dos** detalles)

- **!**

- El alcohol – **una** desventaja

- **?** Drogas

- Remember you can prepare detailed notes in the preparation time and write down *exactly* what you are going to say in the role-play tasks (as well as in response to the three prepared questions on the photo card), so use the 12 minutes wisely.
- Bullet 5 requires any clearly understandable question about drugs and must include a verb, for example: *¿Cuál es tu opinión sobre las drogas?* For a question task, it is also permissible to give a statement using a verb followed by *¿Y a ti?* For example, here, *No me gustan las drogas. ¿Y a ti?* would gain full marks for communication. This way of asking a question will not suit all question tasks, and the question must make sense for the marks to be awarded.

Card A   **Candidate's Photo card**

Part 2

- Look at the photo during the preparation period.

- Make any notes you wish to on an additional piece of paper.

- Your teacher will then ask you questions about the photo and about topics related to **technology in everyday life**.

Your teacher will ask you the following three questions and then **two more questions** which you have not prepared.

- ¿Qué hay en la foto?

- Háblame de la última vez que usaste Internet.

- ¿Cuáles son las ventajas de tener Internet en casa?

> - If you do not understand a particular question, you can ask the teacher-examiner in Spanish, at any time during the exam, to repeat it, using, *Repite, por favor* or *¿Cómo?*, for example.
> - In the Photo card or General Conversation sections, you can also ask the teacher-examiner to re-phrase a question, clarify a particular point or define a particular word: *¿Puede clarificar?* or *¿Qué quiere decir…?* These techniques are known as repair strategies and if you respond to the question successfully after using them, you will be awarded the same mark as if you had understood it originally.

Card B   **Candidate's Photo card**

Part 2

- Look at the photo during the preparation period.

- Make any notes you wish to on an additional piece of paper.

- Your teacher will then ask you questions about the photo and about topics related to **travel and tourism**.

Your teacher will ask you the following three questions and then **two more questions** which you have not prepared.

- ¿Qué hay en la foto?

- ¿Cuáles son las ventajas de ir a la playa en verano?

- ¿Dónde te gustaría ir para tus próximas vacaciones? ¿Por qué?

- If you feel you have made an error while answering one of the questions from the photo card, you should quickly and clearly correct yourself in Spanish. You will **not** be penalised for doing so.
- Avoid using English at any point as this will be considered when the teacher-examiner awards the overall mark for the photo card section.
- Pay close attention to the time frame you need to answer in. The third bullet contains a conditional *te gustaría* ('you would like') and the phrase *próximas vacaciones* ('next holidays'), which means the future tense is required in your answer.

Card C   **Candidate's Photo card**

Part 2

- Look at the photo during the preparation period.

- Make any notes you wish to on an additional piece of paper.

- Your teacher will then ask you questions about the photo and about topics related to **life at school/college**.

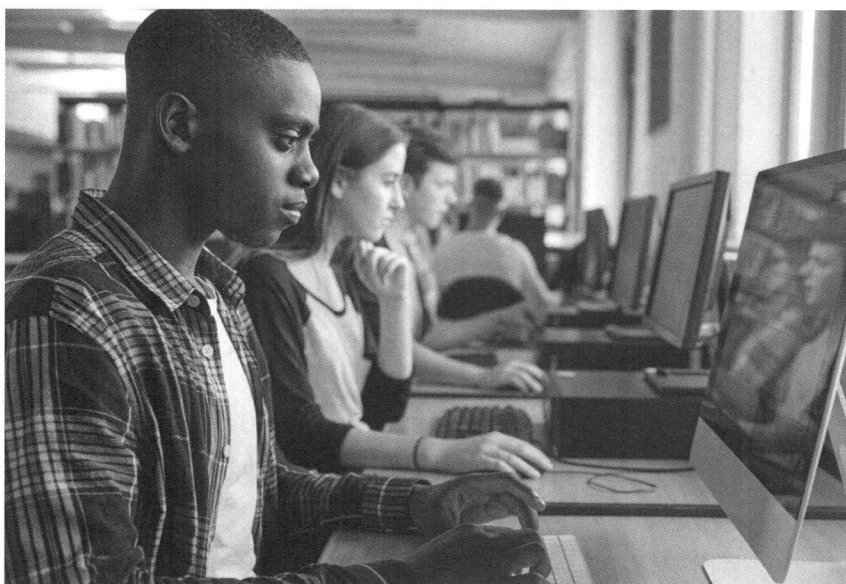

Your teacher will ask you the following three questions and then **two more questions** which you have not prepared.

- ¿Qué hay en la foto?

- En tu opinión, ¿es importante tener una biblioteca en el instituto? ¿Por qué (no)?

- ¿Qué instalaciones habrá en los institutos del futuro?

> - When answering the first question, make sure you describe only what is in the photo, not what there isn't. You may, however, use conjecture if you run out of things to say. For example, you might say something like *Creo que los estudiantes van a comer/almorzar juntos en la cafetería más tarde*.
> - Try to avoid giving opinions on the photo without any justification. For example, *Me encanta la foto* is not a suitable answer on its own, but *Me encanta la foto porque los estudiantes parecen trabajadores* is fine.

GENERAL CONVERSATION

Part 3

The Photo card is followed by a General Conversation. The first part of the conversation will be on a theme nominated by the candidate and the second part on the other theme not covered by the Photo card. The total time for the General Conversation will be between 5 and 7 minutes and a similar amount of time should be spent on each theme. Here is a reminder of the three themes:

- Identity and culture

- Local, national, international and global areas of interest

- Current and future study and employment

The following pages show two examples of the general conversation with accompanying commentary on how these conversations would be marked, followed by tasks.

Conversation 1: Themes 1 and 2

Y ahora la conversación. Empezamos con el tema dos. ¿Qué haces normalmente en verano?
Normalmente voy a Escocia con mis padres. Me quedo en un camping en el norte. Paso tres semanas allí.

¿Qué tiempo hace allí?
Hace buen tiempo porque vamos en julio. Llueve a veces.

Háblame de tus vacaciones del año pasado.
El abril pasado fui a Mallorca en avión.

¿Dónde te alojaste?
–

¿Te quedaste en un hotel?
Sí, me quedé en un hotel de tres estrellas cerca de la playa.

¿Con quién fuiste?
Mis padres.

¿Qué hiciste allí?
Tomé el sol y fui de compras.

¿Qué tal la gastronomía del lugar?
Fue deliciosa. Comí paella todos los días.

¿Por qué te gusta la paella?
Es deliciosa. ¿Te gusta la paella?

Claro que sí. ¿Qué planes futuros tienes para tus próximas vacaciones?
Voy a ir a Brasil.

¿Por qué te gustaría ir a Brasil?
Brasil es tropical y me gusta ir a la playa porque es relajante.

¿Qué otras actividades harás?
–

¿Qué vas a comer o beber en Brasil?
–

Cambiamos de tema y ahora es el tema número uno. ¿Cuál es tu deporte favorito?
Mi deporte favorito es el tenis.

¿Por qué te gusta el tenis?
Es rápido y divertido.

¿Qué actividades vas a hacer este fin de semana?
Este fin de semana voy a ir al cine con mis amigos.

¿Qué película vas a ver?
Me gustan las películas de acción.

¿Prefieres ver las películas en el cine o en casa?
Siempre en el cine porque es mejor.

Pero el cine es caro, ¿no?
Sí, es caro.

¿Qué programas te gustan en la tele?
No soy teleadicto, pero veo un concurso tres o cuatro veces a la semana. Prefiero leer.

Háblame de algo que has leído recientemente.
–

¿Qué vas a leer próximamente?
–

¿Qué aplicaciones usas?
Normalmente uso Instagram y Spotify. Me encanta subir fotos y escuchar música.

¿Qué es lo bueno y lo malo de las redes sociales?
Lo bueno es que son muy divertidas y prácticas.

¿Y lo malo?
A veces son adictivas.

Marks and commentary

	Communication	Range and accuracy of language	Pronunciation and intonation	Spontaneity and fluency	Total
Marks	4/10	4/10	3/5	2/5	**13/30**

This conversation has been given 4 marks for Communication. The responses given are almost always very short and although clear, they do not provide enough detail to reach the 5–6 bracket. There are some questions where an answer isn't even attempted.

4 marks are awarded for Range and accuracy of language. Three time frames are successfully used but there are very few attempts to maintain their use. Furthermore, the vocabulary is generally more suited to the Foundation Tier. For example, *me gusta… porque* is used repeatedly with adjectives such as *divertido*.

Pronunciation and intonation are assumed to be generally good, so gain 3 marks.

For Spontaneity and fluency, 2 marks have been given. Some questions do not receive an answer and many others are basic and hesitant.

> 1. In the conversation find examples of:
>   - the preterite tense
>   - the near future tense.
> 2. Answer the two questions about reading that were not responded to. Check that you have used the correct tense and include as much detail as possible.

Conversation 2: Themes 1 and 2

Y ahora la conversación. Empezamos con el tema dos. ¿Qué haces normalmente en verano?
Normalmente voy a Escocia con mis padres. Vamos a un camping en el norte. Solemos pasar tres semanas allí. Afortunadamente hace buen tiempo por lo general, pero es verdad que llueve a veces. No importa porque el camping tiene piscina cubierta y otras instalaciones, por ejemplo, pistas de tenis.

Háblame de tus vacaciones del año pasado.
El abril pasado fui a Mallorca en avión por primera vez. ¡Fue muy emocionante! Mallorca es una isla preciosa en el mar Mediterráneo y me alojé en un hotel de muy alta calidad cerca de la playa.

¿Qué hiciste en Mallorca?
Todos los días tomé el sol y nadé en el mar. Además, fui a la catedral que se llama La Seu y saqué muchas fotos allí.

¿Qué tal la gastronomía del lugar?
Era deliciosa. Comí muchos mariscos todos los días, por ejemplo, gambas y calamares. Además, comí una ensaimada. Es un postre tradicional.

¿Hablaste mucho español en Mallorca?
Sí, hablé español muchas veces, aunque en los barrios más turísticos hay gente que habla inglés.

¿Qué planes futuros tienes para tus próximas vacaciones?
Voy a ir a Brasil porque es un país fascinante. Me gustaría ir a Río y también a Manaos, una ciudad en la selva tropical.

¿Qué harás allí?
Hablaré portugués y comeré los platos tradicionales del país. Visitaré muchos monumentos.

Cambiamos de tema y ahora es el tema número uno. ¿Cuál es tu deporte favorito?
Actualmente, mi deporte favorito es el tenis, pero juego a otros deportes también, como el golf. No juego a muchos deportes en equipo porque no tengo tiempo.

¿Por qué te gusta tanto el tenis?
A mi modo de ver es un deporte bastante rápido. Además, es ideal para mantenerse en forma.

¿Qué actividades vas a hacer este fin de semana?
Este fin de semana voy a ir al cine con mis amigos. Vamos a un cine a las afueras de la ciudad. Vamos a ver una película de acción y vamos a comer palomitas de maíz.

¿Prefieres ver las películas en el cine o en casa?
Prefiero ir al cine porque la experiencia es mucho mejor. La pantalla es enorme y se puede ir a cenar con amigos después de la película.

Pero el cine es caro, ¿no?
Sí, es caro.

¿Qué programas te gustan en la tele?
No soy un teleadicto, pero veo un concurso tres o cuatro veces a la semana. No veo muchas series ni programas de telerrealidad porque no tengo tiempo. Prefiero leer las noticias en Twitter y hablar sobre política.

Entonces, ¿te gustan las redes sociales?
Me mola Twitter porque es muy eficaz y hay una gran variedad de opiniones. Casi nunca uso Instagram o Facebook porque no me interesa ver fotos.

¿Qué es lo malo de las redes sociales?
Para los estudiantes es evidente que hay problemas de acoso en las redes sociales. Yo no tengo estos problemas, pero tengo amigos que sufren a veces. Es triste, ¿no?

Marks and commentary

	Communication	Range and accuracy of language	Pronunciation and intonation	Spontaneity and fluency	Total
Marks	10/10	10/10	5/5	4/5	**29/30**

This conversation has been given 10 marks for Communication. In contrast to the first conversation, these answers are generally highly detailed, with thoughtful and original content, such as lots of cultural references. The teacher-examiner does not dominate the conversation, which is the case in the first model answer.

10 marks are awarded for Range and accuracy of language. Three time frames are successfully used on multiple occasions, but even more impressively, there are many complex structures and examples of ambitious vocabulary that work very well together. For example, *Yo no tengo estos problemas, pero tengo amigos que sufren a veces. Es triste, ¿no? / La pantalla es enorme y se puede ir a cenar con amigos después de la película.*

Given the quality of the content and language, Pronunciation and intonation are assumed to be excellent, so gain 5 marks.

For Spontaneity and fluency, 4 marks are given. The conversation appears to flow very naturally, although in one instance, a brief spontaneous question from the teacher-examiner receives a very brief and undeveloped answer.

Please see the AQA GCSE Spanish specification for further details of the assessment criteria:
https://filestore.aqa.org.uk/resources/spanish/specifications/AQA-8698-SP-2016.PDF

1. In the conversation find examples of:

   - any Spanish cultural references
   - opinions that are explained.

2. Re-read the two answers to the question *¿Qué haces normalmente en verano?* Compare the answer of model answer 1 with that of model answer 2. Explain why the second answer is better, then write your own answer to the question, using model answer 2 as guidance.

Model answers and mark schemes

AQA GCSE Spanish (9–1)

H

Higher Tier Paper 3 Reading

Time allowed: 1 hour

Instructions

- Answer **all** questions.
- Answer the questions in the spaces provided.
- In **Section A**, answer the questions in **English**. In **Section B**, answer the questions in **Spanish**. In **Section C**, translate the passage into **English**.
- Cross through any work you do not want to be marked.

Information

- The marks for the questions are shown in brackets.
- The maximum mark for this paper is 60.
- You must **not** use a dictionary.

Please note: The Practice Paper questions and answers have not been written or approved by AQA.

Section A   Questions and answers in **English**

0	1

New academic year

You are reading this advice about schools in your Spanish friend's school newsletter.

> **El nuevo curso escolar**
>
> Muchos padres tienen problemas con las solicitudes de colegios de primaria para sus hijos.
>
> Se recomienda a los padres enviar la solicitud antes del mes de enero para tener plaza en septiembre.

> If an example is provided, read it carefully, as it may give you key information that can help you answer the questions that follow. For example, you might work out that *las solicitudes* means 'applications' from the example answer, and the singular form *la solicitud* appears in the following sentence after the verb *enviar* 'to send'.

Answer the question in **English**.

Example   What do many parents have problems with?

Primary school applications.

What does the message recommend parents do?

_____

[1 mark]

0 2   Las Fiestas de la Vendimia, a traditional festival in Valdepeñas, Spain

A group of your Spanish friends are going to the festival.

Read their social media posts.

Write the letter of the correct person in each box.

> - Be aware of key words in the questions such as 'horse' or 'entry' here. Try thinking of words in Spanish that look or sound similar. For example, you might remember *equitación* is 'horse-riding', which is linked to (**D**) *equina* (meaning 'equine').
> - Many words that appear difficult to understand often contain clues within them that can help lead you to the correct answer, for example (**B**) *entrada* > *entrar* ('to enter'); (**E**) *me divierto* > *divertido* ('amusing').

Marisa
Lo mejor de la fiesta es la comida, especialmente en el mercado medieval donde venden carnes y pasteles tradicionales que están muy ricos.

Carlos
Parece que este año el concierto de rock será el evento más concurrido. No quedan entradas.

Elvira
En el mercado medieval no solo hay comida; la ropa y los complementos que venden siempre me llaman la atención.

Raúl
Voy a ir a la feria equina. Nos encanta ver como se mueven al ritmo de la música. ¡Es impresionante!

Gloria
Tengo ganas de ayudar a hacer la paella al aire libre en la Plaza Mayor. ¡Me divierto mucho!

0 2 . 1 Who is looking forward to watching the horse parade? [1 mark]

0 2 . 2 Who fears they may not be able to gain entry to part of the festival? [1 mark]

0 2 . 3 Who enjoys cooking outside? [1 mark]

0 2 . 4 Who is really impressed by the accessories on sale? [1 mark]

<table>
<tr><td>0</td><td>3</td></tr>
</table>

Technology in the home

You are reading this article in a Spanish online magazine.

El salón del futuro

Los salones de las casas españolas van a cambiar para siempre. Antes de fin de año, habrá una aplicación para móvil y tableta desde la que se pueden hacer cosas de casa desde fuera. Encender la televisión, una lámpara o la calefacción será muy fácil, con un clic en el móvil.

Lo bueno de este sistema es que va a ser posible ahorrar energía de manera muy fácil y a buen precio. También se espera que en un futuro no muy lejano la aplicación ofrezca la posibilidad de ver a las mascotas en casa a través de una micro cámara.

Esta aplicación también ofrece información sobre la humedad, la calidad del aire o si tus plantas necesitan agua. Según los expertos, la aplicación es bastante eficaz. Lo malo es que alguien podría engancharse y mirar esta aplicación a todas horas.

Which **four** statements are true?

Write the correct letters in the boxes.

- When completing a reading task that contains a lot of text, make sure you take a positive and attentive approach.
- Read statements A–H carefully and highlight any words or expressions you think will be key before checking the text to see if there is a match. In paragraph 1 for example, *tableta* is mentioned but within the phrase *una aplicación para móvil y tableta*, which should allow you to work out that this app is also for mobile phones. In paragraph 2, the positive phrase *a un buen precio* should lead you to the correct answer on price.

A	The new app will be released before the end of the year.
B	The app is only available on tablet computers.
C	It is possible to control the heating via the app.
D	The app is reasonably priced.
E	Buyers of the app can now see their pets at home via a micro camera.
F	The app cannot yet measure air quality.
G	Experts say that the app is quite unreliable.
H	There is a fear that some users may become addicted.

[4 marks]

| 0 | 4 | **Mexican families**

Your friend shows you an article about large families in Mexico.

Read the article and answer the questions that follow in **English**.

Una familia numerosa

Guzmán y Pablo son dos gemelos adolescentes en una familia numerosa. Además de su padre y su madre, viven con su abuela (que decidió instalarse después de la muerte de su marido), su hermana mayor y dos hermanas pequeñas. Hay problemas de convivencia: ocho personas, solo un baño y falta de privacidad; no obstante, lo bueno es que casi siempre hay una red de apoyo muy fuerte.

Según un reciente estudio, los padres de las familias numerosas están más estresados y duermen menos de seis horas al día. Por el contrario, parece que los niños de este tipo de familias se desarrollan con éxito.

- Remember that the answers are always in order in reading texts, i.e. the answer to question 4.1 will be near the start and the answer to question 4.4 near the end.
- Answer every question and if in doubt, guess something. you may not know that *gemelos* means 'twins', but you can put together the clues *dos… adolescentes en una famila* and *son muy parecidos*.

| 0 | 4 | . | 1 | How are Guzmán and Pablo related?

_____

[1 mark]

| 0 | 4 | . | 2 | For how long has their grandmother lived with them?

_____

[1 mark]

| 0 | 4 | . | 3 | What does the article say is the good thing about living in a large family?

_____

[1 mark]

| 0 | 4 | . | 4 | How does a large family affect a child's development, according to a recent study?

Write   **P**   if the opinion is **positive**

         N   if the opinion is **negative**

       P+N   if the opinion is **positive** and **negative**

[1 mark]

| 0 | 5 |

A questionnaire on free time

Your Argentinian friend, Lucas, has filled in a questionnaire online. Look at the answers he has circled.

¿Qué haces en tu tiempo libre?
Haz este sondeo sobre lo que haces en tu tiempo libre y descubre qué tipo de persona eres.

Example ¿Qué opinas del cine?

A Es entretenido, pero demasiado caro.
B Me aburre un poco.
(C) Suelo ir tres o cuatro veces al mes.

1 ¿Te gusta ver las series en la televisión?

A Raras veces ponen algo que me interesa.
B Solo si mis amigos me recomiendan algo.
(C) ¡Veo todos los episodios de mis series favoritas en un solo día!

2 ¿Cómo reaccionarías si tu amigo cancelara tus planes para el fin de semana?

A Me enfadaría mucho. ¡Qué desastre!
(B) No me importaría porque haríamos algo el siguiente finde.
C Intentaría salir con otro amigo.

3 ¿Qué harías si **no** tuvieras conexión wifi en casa?

(A) Ir inmediatamente a casa de un familiar que la tiene.
B Hacer otra cosa, como leer o preparar la comida.
C Me da igual; no uso Internet.

4 ¿Te consideras deportista?

A No puedo vivir sin visitar el polideportivo semanalmente.
B Un poco, aunque prefiero pasar mi tiempo libre haciendo otra cosa.
(C) Pues… ¡solo juego deportes en mi videoconsola!

This style of question requires you to fully develop your answer. This can mean including information from the questions in the questionnaire as well as from the circled answers. For example, in 5.2, the answer is 'he wouldn't mind if a friend cancelled their weekend plans,' which you can work out from the question and in 5.3, part of the answer is 'if he didn't have an internet connection at home', which also comes from a question.

Example   According to the circled answer, how do you know Lucas enjoys watching films?

He usually goes to the cinema 3 or 4 times a month.

Answer the questions in **English**.

| 0 | 5 | . | 1 | According to the circled answer, how do you know Lucas watches a lot of TV?

_____

_____

[1 mark]

| 0 | 5 | . | 2 | According to the circled answer, how do you know Lucas has a relaxed personality?

_____

_____

[1 mark]

| 0 | 5 | . | 3 | According to the circled answer, how do you know Lucas enjoys being online?

_____

_____

[1 mark]

| 0 | 5 | . | 4 | According to the circled answer, how do you know Lucas is **not** very active?

_____

_____

[1 mark]

0 6   *Luces de Bohemia*, a play by Ramón del Valle-Inclán

Read this extract and answer the questions that follow.

> **MAX:** ¿Eres joven? No puedo verte.
> **EL PRESO:** Soy joven. Treinta años.
> **MAX:** ¿De qué te acusan?
> **EL PRESO:** Es cuento largo. Soy tachado de rebelde… No quise ir a la guerra y levanté una rebelión en la fábrica. Me denunció el patrón, cumplí condena, recorrí el mundo buscando trabajo, y ahora voy por tránsitos, reclamado de no sé qué jueces. Conozco la suerte que me espera: cuatro tiros por intento de fuga.

- Literary texts, especially extracts from plays, are often in the form of a dialogue and contain unfamiliar vocabulary.
- The questions that follow may need you to infer or work out an answer based on evidence. For example, you could conclude that *el preso* means 'prisoner' from a process of elimination. This is a high-level exam skill, so be patient and look for small clues, especially cognates such as *rebelde* 'rebel', *rebelión* 'rebellion', or *denunció* 'denounced'.

Write the correct letter in each box.

0 6 . 1   Which statement best describes the prisoner?

A	He is dirty.
B	He is thirty years old.
C	He is blind.

[1 mark]

0 6 . 2   Which adjectives best describe the prisoner?

A	Young and rebellious.
B	Tall and aggressive.
C	Hard-working and lucky.

[1 mark]

0 6 . 3   What is the prisoner accused of?

A	Starting a riot in a factory.
B	Committing war crimes.
C	Attacking the boss.

[1 mark]

0 6 . 4   What is likely to happen to the prisoner?

A	He will be released.
B	He will receive a long prison sentence.
C	He will be executed.

[1 mark]

| 0 | 7 | **A visit to Granada**

You would like to visit Granada, in the south of Spain, and come across this article online.

Granada, una joya artística que no te puedes perder

- Una visita a **la Alhambra** requiere al menos tres horas. Es un palacio y fortaleza árabe situado sobre la colina de la Sabika, junto al río Darro. Sus orígenes datan del siglo nueve.
- Te encantará probar un '**pionono**': un pastel pequeño y suave con sabor a caramelo que sirven en casi todas las pastelerías de la ciudad.
- La catedral de Granada es especial porque allí está la **Capilla Real**, donde los turistas pueden ver la tumba de los Reyes Católicos, importantísimos en la historia de España.
- Si prefieres los deportes, el club de fútbol de Granada juega en primera división y puedes ir al estadio '**Los Cármenes**' para ver un partido entretenido a buen precio.

Decide if the following statements are true (**T**), false (**F**) or not mentioned (**NM**) in the text.

Write   **T** if the statement is true.

            F if the statement is false.

            NM if the statement is **not mentioned** in the text.

            Write the correct letter(s) in each box.

- The 'NM' ('Not Mentioned') answers often cause confusion among students. If there is not enough evidence in a text to decide whether a statement is true or false, the answer should be 'NM'.
- Be careful: even if a statement appears true, such as 7.3 for example, if it isn't mentioned in the text, it must be 'NM'.
- Use capital letters preferably when answering with a letter, as they are less ambiguous than lower-case letters. If you need to change an answer, cross out the incorrect letter and write the new one(s) clearly.

| 0 | 7 | . | 1 | A visitor should spend no more than three hours in the Alhambra.   **[1 mark]**

| 0 | 7 | . | 2 | You can find *piononos* in every cake shop in Granada.   **[1 mark]**

| 0 | 7 | . | 3 | Granada Cathedral is one of the most visited tourist sites in Spain.   **[1 mark]**

| 0 | 7 | . | 4 | Tickets to watch Granada Football Club are not expensive.   **[1 mark]**

0 8   **Mariola's diet**

You read this interview in a Colombian magazine featuring the famous celebrity, Mariola.

> – **Mariola, ¿consideras que llevas una dieta equilibrada?**
>
> – A menos que haya alguna fiesta de cumpleaños u otra ocasión especial, yo evito las grasas. Suelo comer mucha fruta y verdura, sobre todo plátanos y zanahorias.
>
> – **¿Qué cambiarías de tu dieta?**
>
> – No sé. Quizás, dentro de dos o tres años comería más mariscos, como gambas, por ejemplo.
>
> – **¿Has probado otras cocinas internacionales?**
>
> – He viajado a Italia con mi familia y comí mucha pasta allí. Nunca he comido sushi, pero tengo ganas de probarlo en el futuro.

Answer the questions in **English**.

- Remember that the questions follow the order of the text, so the answer to 8.1 is likely to be found in the first interview question and so forth.
- Grammatical accuracy is often important to gain the marks and you will need to show understanding of various tenses in your answers. For example, in 8.2, the conditional *comería* ('I would eat') is key when referring to *mariscos* ('seafood'), and in 8.3, the negative construction *nunca* in front of the perfect tense *he comido* ('I have eaten') changes the meaning of the phrase entirely.

0 8 . 1   Name two food groups in Mariola's current diet and the two specific foods she eats most of all.

_____

_____

[1 mark]

0 8 . 2   What would Mariola change about her diet?

_____

_____

[1 mark]

0 8 . 3   What does Mariola say about sushi?

_____

_____

[1 mark]

| 0 | 9 |

Interview with a sportswoman

You read this interview in a Spanish magazine featuring famous handball player, Silvia Torres.

–¿En qué momento supo usted que este deporte era su mayor afición?	– Creo que cuando tenía diez años y empecé a jugar en el equipo de mi instituto, todo cambió. Mi madre me aconsejaba mucho porque en su juventud jugaba al polo acuático a un nivel alto.
–¿Disfruta de su posición como portera?	– Se dice que las porteras no jugamos tanto como el resto de jugadoras y que no somos tan atléticas. A mi modo de ver, no es verdad. Pienso que es la posición más exigente.
–¿Cree usted que el balonmano es un deporte popular en España?	– Por supuesto. Actualmente la liga nacional de balonmano mueve mucho dinero y cada vez viene más gente a los partidos. Ojalá que la participación juvenil en este deporte siga creciendo en el futuro.

- This is an extended text and with only 1 mark on offer per question, you can assume there is extra information that can be disregarded. For example, in 9.2, focus on the information that comes after *A mi modo de ver* ('In my opinion') and *Pienso* ('I think') as you are asked for Silvia's description of the position of goalkeeper, and not other people's.
- In 9.3, the conjunction *Ojalá que…* ('Let's hope…') points you in the right direction of the answer.

Answer the questions in **English**.

| 0 | 9 | . | 1 | Why is Silvia grateful to her mother?

_____

_____

[1 mark]

| 0 | 9 | . | 2 | How does Silvia describe the position of goalkeeper?

_____

_____

[1 mark]

| 0 | 9 | . | 3 | What is Silvia's hope for the future?

_____

_____

[1 mark]

Section B   Questions and answers in **Spanish**

| 1 | 0 | *Pepita Jiménez*, una novela de Juan Valera

Lee el extracto.

> Don Gumersindo, muy aseado y cuidadoso de su persona, era un viejo que no inspiraba repugnancia.
> Las prendas de su sencillo vestuario estaban algo raídas, y de tiempo inmemorial se le conocía la misma capa, el mismo chaquetón y los mismos pantalones y chaleco.
> Don Gumersindo tenía excelentes cualidades: era afable, servicial, compasivo, y se desvivía por complacer y ser útil a cualquier persona, aunque le costase trabajo, desvelos y fatiga.
> Ya he dicho que era tío de la Pepita. Cuando frisaba en los ochenta años, iba ella a cumplir los dieciséis.

Termina las frases con la palabra correcta.

Escribe la letra correcta en cada casilla.

| 1 | 0 | . | 1 | Don Gumersindo era una persona…

A	repugnante.
B	higiénica.
C	desordenada.

[1 mark]

| 1 | 0 | . | 2 | Don Gumersindo nunca cambiaba su…

A	expresión.
B	opinión.
C	ropa.

[1 mark]

| 1 | 0 | . | 3 | Don Gumersindo se comportaba de manera muy atenta con…

A	todo el mundo.
B	la familia real.
C	sus trabajadores.

[1 mark]

1 0 . 4   Pepita tenía…

A	catorce años.
B	ochenta años.
C	dieciséis anos.

[1 mark]

- Don't be put off by literary texts even when you feel that you cannot understand them very well. Always be on the lookout for synonyms as they will often lead you to the correct answer, *cuidadoso > higiénica*, for example.
- Avoid distractors – the most obvious option is rarely the right one! In 10.1, you might link *repugnante* to *repugnancia*, but fail to spot the negative *no* in the text.
- Look for clues, such as the repetition of *mismo/misma/mismos* ('same'), followed by words that appear to be clothes items (*chaquetón, pantalones*). This may help lead you to the correct answer for 10.2 – what did Don Gumersindo never change?

1 1   **El mundo laboral**

Completa el texto usando palabras de la lista.

Escribe la letra correcta en cada casilla.

A	posibilidades
B	educación
C	falta
D	inteligencia
E	mayoría

> - These gap-fill tasks often require a very strong knowledge of higher-level vocabulary. The challenge here is to understand the meaning of the sentences so that you can identify the correct feminine noun to insert.
> - Aim to work out the meaning gradually from context and by ruling out the more unlikely options.
> - Start by looking carefully at the words on either side of each gap and 'testing out' each noun to see if one sounds sensible.

1 1 . 1   La causa más importante del paro en España es la ☐ de trabajos en el sector económico secundario.

[1 mark]

1 1 . 2   Es posible asistir a cursos de idiomas para mejorar las ☐ de encontrar trabajo.

[1 mark]

1 1 . 3   Es evidente que la ☐ de los desempleados lleva sin trabajar menos de tres años seguidos.

[1 mark]

1 2   **Los exámenes finales**

Ves esta página en una revista, en la que tres jóvenes hablan sobre los estudios.

Para sacar buenas notas, empiezo la revisión dos meses antes, poco a poco. Me hace falta un horario de revisión – para mí, es muy útil.

Adela

Las estadísticas muestran que la asistencia y la puntualidad son la clave más importante para sacar las mejores notas. Por eso, aconsejo que nunca llegues tarde al instituto.

Basilio

Mi secreto es pasar tiempo en la biblioteca, porque es un lugar silencioso donde estudiar sin molestias. Lo malo es que a veces hay alguien que olvida apagar el teléfono móvil y recibe una llamada.

Carmen

Contesta a las preguntas en **español**.

- Only include relevant material in your answers as you can lose marks by adding incorrect information.
- There are clues in the questions that can help you locate the answers in the text. For example, in 12.1, *necesita* is synonymous with *hace falta* ('need'). In 12.2, *consejo* ('advice') is linked to *aconsejar* ('to advise'). And in 12.3, you are looking for an advantage (*ventaja*), so the information is unlikely to come directly after the phrase *lo malo es* ('the bad thing is…').

1 2 . 1   ¿Qué necesita Adela?

_____

[1 mark]

1 2 . 2   ¿Qué consejo da Basilio?

_____

[1 mark]

1 2 . 3   ¿Cuál es la ventaja de la biblioteca para Carmen?

_____

[1 mark]

| 1 | 3 | **El cambio climático y los países latinoamericanos** |

Te interesa el cambio climático y lees estos titulares en una página web.

	Impacto del cambio climático en América Latina
A	En Chile, el aumento del nivel de agua en la costa amenaza a la población, sobre todo en Santiago, la capital.
B	En Argentina, los glaciares del sur desaparecen y los pingüinos no tienen un hábitat seguro para reproducirse.
C	En Perú, la sequía en la ciudad de Lima causa deficiencias en el servicio de agua potable en siete barrios de la capital.
D	En Bogotá, la capital de Colombia, la subida de la temperatura media provoca que los pájaros mueran o emigren a otros climas más frescos.
E	En Panamá, la contaminación del aire en la capital produce alergias y problemas respiratorios en los habitantes.
F	Bolivia sufre incendios devastadores en el Amazonas que acaban con cultivos de frutas y verduras.

Tus amigos están interesados en ayudar a las víctimas del cambio climático.

¿Dónde deben ir?

Escribe la letra correcta en cada casilla.

- For these types of reading activity, use a process of elimination by first identifying key words or phrases in statements 1–4. This should lead you efficiently to the correct answer, but don't guess too soon!
- In 13.1, you might consider *lugares más fríos* ('coldest places') important, and after scanning the headings A–F, earmark B, as it mentions *glaciares*, an obvious cognate.
- Watch out for distractors: in 13.4, you might connect *agua* with heading A, as *agua* is mentioned there, but fail to spot the negative *no* in the question text. The correct answer is in fact C, where there is a drought (*la sequía*), i.e. lack of water.

| 1 | 3 |. | 1 | Me interesa visitar los lugares más fríos del mundo. | | **[1 mark]** |

| 1 | 3 |. | 2 | Siempre he querido salvar a las aves que están en peligro. | | **[1 mark]** |

| 1 | 3 |. | 3 | He trabajado de bombero y quiero apagar fuegos. | | **[1 mark]** |

| 1 | 3 |. | 4 | Quiero ayudar a los ciudadanos que no tienen agua en la capital. | | **[1 mark]** |

1 4   Un artículo en Internet

Lee este artículo y responde a las preguntas en **español**.

Los divorcios rápidos

Se dice que la solución más rápida a un matrimonio que no funciona es el divorcio. Tradicionalmente, el proceso del divorcio era lento y poco claro, pero ya hay un tipo de 'divorcio express' que puede solucionar el problema matrimonial en unos días. Por ejemplo, 'Abogados Garón' anuncia en su página web que ofrece 'el mejor servicio de divorcio rápido en Madrid'.

El jefe de Garón, Ángel Vicente Martínez, explica que cuando la separación es amistosa y sin complicaciones, la pareja puede acceder a este servicio para terminar con el proceso de manera muy eficaz. También admite que hay otros requisitos para este tipo de separación legal, como no tener hijos menores de edad.

- When answering questions in Spanish, avoid writing in full sentences – just provide the relevant information from the text. Don't copy whole chunks of Spanish as you won't be awarded the mark if you include the wrong answer as well as the correct one.
- When searching for the answer in the stimulus text, it can come *after* the key word or phrase from the question, but also *before* it. For example, in 14.2, the answer can be found in the text after the key word(s) *su página web que ofrece…*. In 14.3, the answer comes before the key word *acceder (a)…* from the question.

1 4 . 1   ¿Cuáles eran los problemas de un divorcio tradicional?

_____

[1 mark]

1 4 . 2   Según su página web, ¿qué ofrece Abogados Garón?

_____

[1 mark]

1 4 . 3   Según Ángel Vicente Martínez, ¿cómo debería ser la separación para acceder a un divorcio rápido?

_____

[1 mark]

1 4 . 4   ¿Qué no se debe tener si quieres un divorcio rápido?

_____

[1 mark]

Section C   Translation into **English**

1 5   Your Spanish exchange partner sends you this message.

Translate it into **English** for a friend.

> Me gusta asistir a partidos de baloncesto. Actualmente mi jugadora favorita es Marta Xargay. Juega al baloncesto profesional desde hace diez años y ha participado en muchos campeonatos internacionales. Por todas partes de Europa el baloncesto femenino es cada vez más popular y estrellas como Marta juegan un papel importante. Pronto iré a su próximo partido a las afueras de mi ciudad.

[9 marks]

- When translating into English, be as precise as possible, and look out for false friends, i.e. words that look like English words, but have a different meaning! For example, *asistir* means 'to attend', not 'to assist' and *actualmente* means 'currently', not 'actually'.
- When you have finished your translation, read it again to make sure that it makes sense. You would only ever hear the phrase 'women's basketball' for instance, never 'feminine basketball'.

END OF QUESTIONS

Answers and mark schemes

AQA GCSE Spanish (9–1)

Higher Tier Paper 4 Writing

Time allowed: 1 hour 15 minutes

Instructions

- You must answer **three** questions.
- You must answer **either** Question 1.1 **or** Question 1.2. Do not answer both of these questions.
- You must answer **either** Question 2.1 **or** Question 2.2. Do not answer both of these questions.
- You must answer Question 3.
- Answer all questions in **Spanish**.
- Answer the questions in the spaces provided.
- Cross through any work you do not want to be marked.

Information

- The marks for the questions are shown in brackets.
- The maximum mark for this paper is 60.
- You must **not** use a dictionary during this test.
- In order to score the highest marks for Question 1.1/Question 1.2, you must write something about each bullet point. You must use a variety of vocabulary and structures and include your opinions.
- In order to score the highest marks for Question 2.1/Question 2.2, you must write something about both bullet points. You must use a variety of vocabulary and structures and include your opinions and reasons.

Please note: The Practice Paper questions and answers have not been written or approved by AQA.

Answer **either** Question 1.1 **or** Question 1.2.
You must **not** answer **both** of these questions.

EITHER Question 1.1

`0` `1` . `1` Ves una página web con el título, 'Cómo cuidar de tu barrio'.

Decides escribir sobre tu barrio.

Menciona:

- tus sitios favoritos de tu barrio

- qué hiciste en tu barrio la semana pasada

- qué se debe hacer para cuidar bien de tu barrio

- dónde te gustaría vivir en el futuro.

Escribe aproximadamente **90** palabras en **español**.
Responde a todos los aspectos de la pregunta.

[16 marks]

- Use the bullet points carefully; try to answer all four bullet points in order and tick them off on the exam paper as you do so.
- Identify which bullet points target which time frame and check that your tenses are accurate. For example, the second bullet contains the preterite *hiciste*, so you need to use the past; the fourth bullet contains the conditional *te gustaría*.
- Look out for bullet points that offer language that you can use in your answer. For example, the third bullet point *qué se debe hacer para cuidar bien de tu barrio* gives you an ideal start to a sentence: *Para cuidar bien de mi barrio…* (to say 'my neighbourhood', change the possessive pronoun *tu* (your) to *mi* (my)).

OR Question 1.2

`0` `1` . `2` Tu amiga española, Sara, te pregunta sobre las Navidades en tu país.

Escríbele un email.

Menciona:

- qué hiciste el día de Navidad del año pasado

- tu opinión sobre las Navidades

- qué fiestas te gustan más

- qué fiesta española o latinoamericana te gustaría ver en persona.

Escribe aproximadamente **90** palabras en **español**.
Responde a todos los aspectos de la pregunta.

[16 marks]

- When revising for your writing exam, learn a handful of impressive expressions and opinions. Opinions are needed in the second and third bullets and you will gain higher marks if you include a variety of verbs and vocabulary in your answer: *me encanta, me chifla, odio, prefiero* rather than just *(no) me gusta*.
- Identify any language that can be re-used in your answer. The fourth bullet gives you a possible sentence starter, if you change the reflexive pronoun *te* (you) to *me* (I): *La fiesta española que me gustaría ver en persona es…*

Answer **either** Question 2.1 **or** Question 2.2.
You must **not** answer **both** of these questions.

EITHER Question 2.1

`0 2 . 1` Durante tus vacaciones en México, escribes un email a Fabio, tu amigo español.

Menciona:

- un día desastroso que tuviste

- una experiencia cultural que vas a tener.

Escribe aproximadamente **150** palabras en **español**. Responde a los dos aspectos de la pregunta.

[32 marks]

- Make sure that your answers to each point are fully relevant. Here, for example, the focus needs to be on the problem(s) on holiday. Plan the content of your answer briefly first to avoid going off track.
- Only two time frames are targeted in the bullets, but try to use a wide range of tenses in your answer.
- Try to include: infinitive constructions such as those introduced by prepositions (*después de, antes de, al*); adjectives (*es fácil hacerlo*); nouns (*tengo la intención de salir*) and verbs (*prefiero ir, suelo ir*); connectives such as *porque, dado que, ya que, así que*.

OR Question 2.2

`0 2 . 2` Tu gimnasio local quiere artículos para su revista digital con el título 'Juventud Sana'.

Decides escribir un artículo con esta información.

Menciona:

- una semana activa que tuviste recientemente

- tus recomendaciones para una vida sana.

Escribe aproximadamente **150** palabras en **español**. Responde a los dos aspectos de la pregunta.

[32 marks]

- For the first bullet, you need to mention an active week that you had recently, so consider structuring your answer with days of the week as time markers, such as *el lunes, el martes, el miércoles* etc. Don't just write in the present tense about your opinion of different types of activity, as this will be considered largely irrelevant.
- If you have time at the end of the exam, check your verbs and spellings in your answer as carefully as possible; the criteria for marks for Accuracy in Higher Question 2 refer specifically to 'verb and tense formations' and how correct these are.

0 3   Translate the following passage into **Spanish**.

> Next week, I am going to visit the coast. My cousin lives there in a modern house near to the beach. I love going out with her because she is fun and generous. Last July, we swam in the sea and in the evening, we had dinner in an open-air restaurant. How relaxing!

[12 marks]

- Practise translations as much as possible. After a while, you will find that the same high-frequency words, phrases and even general vocabulary come up regularly.
- Days of the week, months of the year and time phrases will often feature, for example: *hoy, ayer, mañana, por la mañana/tarde/noche, la semana que viene, la semana pasada, ahora, después, durante, todo el tiempo* etc.
- If you do not know a word or phrase, try to think of an alternative that might work in its place, as it may still score you a mark. You may not know 'next to' *(al lado de)* for instance, but remember the phrase 'near to' *(cerca de)*, which would be credited, whereas leaving it blank will not get you any marks.

END OF QUESTIONS

Model answers and mark schemes

AQA GCSE Spanish (9–1)

H

Higher Tier Paper 1 Listening

Time allowed: 45 minutes
(including 5 minutes' reading time before the test)

You will need no other materials.
The pauses are pre-recorded for this test.

Information
- The marks for the questions are shown in brackets. The maximum mark for this paper is 50.
- You must **not** use a dictionary.

Advice
This is what you should do for each item.
- After the question number is announced, there will be a pause to allow you to read the instructions and questions.
- Listen carefully to the recording and read the questions again.
- Listen to the recording again, and then answer the questions.
- When the next question is about to start you will hear a bleep.
- You may write at any time during the test.
- In **Section A**, answer the questions in **English**. In **Section B**, answer the questions in **Spanish**.
- You must answer all the questions in the spaces provided. Do not write on blank pages.
- Write neatly and put down all the information you are asked to give.
- **You must not ask questions or interrupt during the test.**
- You have five minutes to read through the question paper. You may make notes during this time. You may turn to the questions now.
- **The test starts now.**

Listen to the audio

Please note: The Practice Paper questions and answers have not been written or approved by AQA.

Section A   Questions and answers in **English**

School facilities

Your Spanish friend, Ernesto, is describing his school.

Answer in **English**.

What aspect does he **like** about the…

> The distractor in this type of question is heard at the start of each utterance. Remain patient and make sure your answer is brief and accurate.

Example   canteen?

the food

0 1   classrooms?

_____

[1 mark]

0 2   hall?

_____

[1 mark]

0 3   sports facilities?

_____

[1 mark]

In the news

You are listening to the following news items on a Mexican radio station.

A	Recycling facility closure affects jobs
B	Underground line reopens after repair
C	Tragedy hits local theme park
D	Film premiere location revealed
E	Car accidents on the rise
F	Traffic misery continues
G	Tree planting boost for city park

Match the headline to each item of news. Write the correct letter in each box.

0 4 [ ] **[1 mark]**

0 5 [ ] **[1 mark]**

0 6 [ ] **[1 mark]**

0 7 [ ] **[1 mark]**

0 8 [ ] **[1 mark]**

Opinions about a new school in Tenerife

Listen to your friends, Natalia and Luis, talking about their new school building.

What are their opinions on the new school's facilities?

Write   **P** if the opinion is positive.

       N if the opinion is negative.

       P+N if the opinion is positive and negative.

0 9   Natalia

The library [ ]   and the laboratories [ ]

[2 marks]

1 0   Luis

The swimming pool [ ]   and the canteen [ ]

[2 marks]

A visit to Madrid

Your Argentinian friends, Miguel and Susana, are telling you about their recent visit to Madrid.

What did they like and dislike about their trip?

A	Night life
B	Food
C	Sport
D	Accommodation
E	Architecture
F	Locals
G	Public transport
H	Parks
I	Shop assistants
J	Weather

Write the correct letter in each box.

Answer **both** parts of the question.

1 1 . 1 Miguel likes… ☐ ☐ **[2 marks]**

1 1 . 2 Miguel dislikes… ☐ ☐ **[2 marks]**

Answer **both** parts of the question.

1 2 . 1 Susana likes… ☐ ☐ **[2 marks]**

1 2 . 2 Susana dislikes… ☐ ☐ **[2 marks]**

Mobile phone use in schools

You are visiting a school in Cádiz and a teacher explains to you the school's policy on mobile phone use.

> • Be careful about using your own experience to answer questions on topics you may be familiar with, such as this one.
> • It is unlikely that the correct answer will be the most obvious one. Listen carefully and make no assumptions.

1 3 Mobile phone use is not allowed…

A	before 9am.
B	in class or at lunchtime.
C	at any time.

Write the correct letter in the box. [ ] **[1 mark]**

1 4 Some teachers say mobile phones…

A	can have a positive impact on education.
B	are a constant distraction.
C	result in too much online activity.

Write the correct letter in the box. [ ] **[1 mark]**

1 5 Parents are now able to…

A	speak to teachers directly via a special app.
B	monitor what homework their child has been set.
C	receive regular comments on their child's progress.

Write the correct letter in the box. [ ] **[1 mark]**

| 1 | 6 | **Social issues** |

You are listening to a podcast where people are discussing social issues that concern them in Spanish cities.

For each speaker, choose their area of concern.

Write the correct letter in each box.

A	Poverty
B	Unemployment
C	Obesity
D	Drug addiction
E	Crime

Answer **all** parts of the question.

| 1 | 6 | . | 1 | Beatriz | ☐ | **[1 mark]** |

| 1 | 6 | . | 2 | Nia | ☐ | **[1 mark]** |

| 1 | 6 | . | 3 | Alberto | ☐ | **[1 mark]** |

| 1 | 7 | **Job prospects in Chile**

You are listening to a podcast interview with Chilean employment expert, Marcela Fernández.

Answer **all** parts of the questions in **English**.

> Make sure you try to answer all questions. Those that require answers in English are sometimes left blank by students, but many require only a brief answer. Stay positive!

| 1 | 7 | . | 1 | What does Marcela say should be the government's main priority?

_____

[1 mark]

| 1 | 7 | . | 2 | What does Marcela predict will happen if changes are not made?

_____

[1 mark]

| 1 | 7 | . | 3 | What has the company Telefónica recently done?

_____

[1 mark]

| 1 | 8 | **Interview with Marcela (continued)**

What **two** points does Marcela state in response to the interviewer's question?

Complete the sentences in **English**.

| 1 | 8 | . | 1 | The Chilean government should abolish university fees and…

_____

[1 mark]

| 1 | 8 | . | 2 | The possible consequence of this is that…

_____

[1 mark]

Volunteering in Spain

You hear your Spanish friend, Isabel, talking to her friends about volunteering in the local community.

Complete the sentences in **English**.

> In some listening tasks, you may hear the polite form of address *usted*, or the *vosotros* plural command. If so, don't panic, listen to the details you require to answer the question rather than looking at it as a grammar test.

1 9   This weekend, Isabel needs volunteers to…

_____

[1 mark]

2 0   At the end of the day, Isabel would like the volunteers to…

_____

[1 mark]

An interview with the gymnast, Juan Vega

You are watching a Spanish TV programme in which Guatemalan gymnast Juan Vega is being interviewed.

What questions does the interviewer ask him?

Answer in **English**.

Example <u>Do you miss your family when you compete?</u>

2 1

[1 mark]

2 2

[1 mark]

2 3

[1 mark]

2 4

[1 mark]

Exam preparation

You are listening to a podcast on a Spanish radio station in which a psychologist discusses effective exam technique.

Answer **all** parts of the question in **English**.

> Use the lines provided beneath the question as guidance for how much you should write. Most answers require only a short response, but two lines will need more detail.

2 5   What **two** things should a student do immediately before the exam?

1

_____

_____

2

_____

_____

[2 marks]

2 6   Name **one** benefit of keeping calm during an exam.

_____

_____

[1 mark]

Section B   Questions and answers in **Spanish**

El tiempo libre

Estás con tus dos amigos, Valeria y Santiago, que hablan de su tiempo libre.

¿De qué hablan y cuándo?

Completa la tabla en **español**.

2 7   Valeria

En el pasado	Ahora	En el futuro
leer novelas de aventuras		

[**2 marks**]

2 8   Santiago

En el pasado	Ahora	En el futuro
	seguir la moda	

[**2 marks**]

Las experiencias laborales

Escuchas al director de un instituto que habla sobre experiencias laborales.

Escribe cada trabajo que menciona.

Contesta en **español**.

Ejemplo   mecánico

2 9

_____

[**1 mark**]

3 0

_____

[**1 mark**]

3 1

_____

[**1 mark**]

La prima de Pedro

Tu amigo español, Pedro, te habla de su prima Lola.

> For challenging questions, it is particularly important to listen carefully both times and remember, you won't need to get every answer right for a great exam performance.

3 2 ¿Qué dice Pedro de su prima?

Selecciona las **dos** frases correctas.

A	Está estudiando en la universidad.
B	No tiene la intención de trabajar.
C	Quiere vivir con sus padres.
D	Estudiar es su pasión.

Escribe la letra correcta en cada casilla. [2 marks]

3 3 ¿Qué van a hacer los padres de Lola?

A	Perdonarla.
B	Aconsejarla.
C	Castigarla.

Escribe la letra correcta en la casilla. [1 mark]

END OF QUESTIONS

Answers and mark schemes

AQA GCSE Spanish (9–1)

PRACTICE PAPER

H

Higher Tier Paper 2 Speaking

Time allowed: 10–12 minutes
(+12 minutes' supervised preparation time)

Candidate's material – Role-play and Photo card

Instructions

- During the preparation time you must prepare the Role-play card and Photo card given to you.
- You may make notes during the preparation time on the paper provided by your teacher-examiner. Do not write on the stimulus cards.
- Hand your notes and both stimulus cards to the teacher-examiner before the General Conversation.
- You must ask the teacher-examiner at least one question in the General Conversation.

Information

- The test will last a maximum of 12 minutes and will consist of a Role-play (approximately 2 minutes) and a Photo card (approximately 3 minutes), followed by a General Conversation (between 5 and 7 minutes) based on your nominated Theme and the remaining Theme which has not been covered in the Photo card.
- You must **not** use a dictionary at any time during the test. This includes the preparation time.

Teacher Part

Please note: The Practice Paper questions and answers have not been written or approved by AQA.

ROLE-PLAY 1

CANDIDATE'S ROLE

Part 1

Instructions to candidates

Your teacher will play the part of a job interviewer in Spain and will speak first.

You should address the interviewer as *usted*.

When you see this – **!** – you will have to respond to something you have not prepared.

When you see this – **?** – you will have to ask a question.

Estás hablando con un entrevistador / una entrevistadora para un puesto de trabajo en España.

- Tu trabajo ahora (**dos** detalles)

- **!**

- Trabajo en España (**dos** razones)

- **?** Horario

- Tus planes para el futuro

- Look out for words in the bullet points that alert you to the tense you need to use: bullet 1 mentions *ahora* ('now') so you will need the present tense; bullet 5 mentions *el futuro*, so you need a future tense.
- You are asked for two details in bullet 1, but remember, it is acceptable to use just one verb, for example: *soy camarero* (first detail) *en un restaurante italiano* (second detail).
- For each bullet point, all of the language you use is marked up to the point that the task is accomplished. Anything you say in relation to the task after that point is ignored. If you first say something which is wrong and follow it with a correct response to the bullet point, only 1 mark out of 2 is awarded for communication and the incorrect part of the message is also considered when awarding the language mark. This means that for each bullet point, your first utterance is very important!

ROLE-PLAY 2

CANDIDATE'S ROLE

Part 1

Instructions to candidates

Your teacher will play the part of your Chilean friend and will speak first.

You should address your friend as *tú*.

When you see this – **!** – you will have to respond to something you have not prepared.

When you see this – **?** – you will have to ask a question.

Estás hablando con tu amigo chileno / tu amiga chilena sobre la familia y los amigos.

- Familia numerosa – **un** aspecto positivo y **un** aspecto negativo

- Padres – relación

- **!**

- Tus planes con tus amigos el fin de semana que viene (**dos** detalles)

- **?** Actividades con amigos

- At Higher Tier, the role-plays ask for more details than at Foundation Tier, so try to answer each bullet point in full, checking your verb formation, particularly in past tense responses.
- Carefully read through the role-play scenario so you are clear about the situation or context. Here, you are talking to a friend about family/friendships and bullets 4 and 5 mention *planes* and *actividades*, so the topic is evidently free time.
- Use the preparation time to think about what you might be asked in the surprise (!) question: here it is likely to be something related to family or free time. Remember that there may even be two elements to it. The second element is often *¿Por qué?*, where you are asked to justify an opinion you've just been asked to give, with a reason.

ROLE-PLAY 3

CANDIDATE'S ROLE

Part 1

Instructions to candidates

Your teacher will play the part of an assistant in a Spanish train station and will speak first.

You should address the assistant as *usted*.

When you see this – **!** – you will have to respond to something you have not prepared.

When you see this – **?** – you will have to ask a question.

Estás hablando con un empleado / una empleada en una estación de tren sobre un viaje.

- Excursión a Barcelona – número de billetes y cuándo
- **!**
- **?** Coste del viaje
- Viajar en tren – tu opinión (**dos** detalles)
- Tu último viaje en tren (**dos** detalles)

- Whereas in the Photo card and Conversation sections of your speaking exam you are encouraged to use ambitious language and detail, in the role-play section this is not required. Errors can cost you marks for both communication and knowledge and use of language, so keep it simple and don't go beyond the requirements of the task.
- The most challenging aspect of the role-play is answering a bullet point that refers to either past or future events. Here, bullet 5 mentions *tu último viaje en tren* ('your last train journey') so you will need to use the past tense.
- To help you make sure the verb forms you use are correct, try to learn the 'I' form of a range of common verbs in both a past and future tense.

Card A   **Candidate's Photo card**

Part 2

- Look at the photo during the preparation period.

- Make any notes you wish to on an additional piece of paper.

- Your teacher will then ask you questions about the photo and about topics related to **technology in everyday life**.

Your teacher will ask you the following three questions and then **two more questions** which you have not prepared.

- ¿Qué hay en la foto?

- ¿Qué es lo bueno y lo malo de usar el móvil todos los días?

- ¿Cómo sería tu vida sin móvil?

- Answering the two unprepared questions can be very daunting. Make sure you know common question words such as *¿cuándo?, ¿cuántos?, ¿cuál?, ¿dónde?, ¿quién?, ¿cómo?, ¿por qué?* and *¿qué?* Keep calm, listen carefully and take your time.
- You can ask the teacher-examiner to repeat the question, but remember to do so in Spanish: *¿Puedes repetir, por favor?*
- For a mark in the top band, you will have to answer and develop at least three (i.e. 'most') answers, as well as answer all five questions clearly and give and explain at least one opinion.

Card B	**Candidate's Photo card**
Part 2	

- Look at the photo during the preparation period.

- Make any notes you wish to on an additional piece of paper.

- Your teacher will then ask you questions about the photo and about topics related to **home, town, neighbourhood and region**.

Your teacher will ask you the following three questions and then **two more questions** which you have not prepared.

- ¿Qué hay en la foto?

- ¿Prefieres hacer las compras en un centro comercial o en Internet? ¿Por qué?

- ¿Qué hiciste en tu ciudad el fin de semana pasado?

- There is a time limit of three minutes in the Photo card section of the Higher speaking exam, but it is unlikely that you will need all of this time to answer the five questions. Nevertheless, in the 12 minutes' allocated preparation time, you will need to spend more time on the Photo card than the role-play.
- Try to prepare answers of at least three sentences for each bullet using a verb in each one. Write detailed notes and try to anticipate what the surprise questions might be.

Card C   **Candidate's Photo card**

Part 2

- Look at the photo during the preparation period.

- Make any notes you wish to on an additional piece of paper.

- Your teacher will then ask you questions about the photo and about topics related to **jobs, career choices and ambitions**.

Your teacher will ask you the following three questions and then **two more questions** which you have not prepared.

- ¿Qué hay en la foto?

- ¿Cuáles son las desventajas de trabajar en una oficina?

- ¿Qué trabajo te gustaría hacer en el futuro?

- Make sure you do lots of photo card practice. Over time, you will notice that photo cards on the same topic area often have similar questions and they will all have at least one question in either a past or future tense. It pays to practise using past and future tenses so that you can answer questions more readily.
- It is much easier to answer questions similar to those you have practised before than have to think of something new in the limited preparation time you have before you enter the exam!

GENERAL CONVERSATION

Part 3

The Photo card is followed by a General Conversation. The first part of the conversation will be on a theme nominated by the candidate and the second part on the other theme not covered by the Photo card. The total time for the General Conversation will be between 5 and 7 minutes and a similar amount of time should be spent on each theme. Here is a reminder of the three themes:

- Identity and culture

- Local, national, international and global areas of interest

- Current and future study and employment

The following pages show two examples of the general conversation with accompanying commentary on how these conversations would be marked, followed by tasks.

Conversation 1: Themes 2 and 3

Y ahora la conversación. Empezamos con el tema dos. ¿Dónde vives?
Vivo en una ciudad. En el pasado vivía en un pueblo.

¿Cómo era ese pueblo?
No sé. Era pequeño.

¿Cómo es la ciudad donde vives ahora?
Es bastante grande y me gusta porque es interesante.

Y ¿qué no te gusta de tu ciudad?
A veces es un poco sucia y peligrosa. Es pequeña también.

¿Por qué es peligrosa? ¿Hay problemas sociales?
Sí, muchos.

¿Por ejemplo?
–

Háblame de tu casa.
Vivo en un piso moderno en el centro de la ciudad. Mi piso tiene dos dormitorios bonitos.

¿Cómo es tu dormitorio?
Mi dormitorio es grande, moderno y muy interesante.

¿Qué hay en tu dormitorio?
Hay una cama blanca, una alfombra amarilla y a la derecha del armario hay una estantería.

¿Dónde te gustaría vivir en el futuro?
Me gustaría vivir en Londres porque es más interesante y es muy grande también.

¿Cuáles son las desventajas de vivir en Londres?
–

Cambiamos de tema y ahora es el tema número tres. ¿Qué asignaturas estudias?
Estudio ocho asignaturas, prefiero la geografía.

¿Por qué prefieres la geografía?
Me gusta viajar.

¿Hay alguna asignatura que no te guste?
Odio la educación física a causa del profesor.

¿Cómo son los profesores de tu instituto?
Depende. Mis profesores de inglés y de geografía son muy interesantes.

Y ¿cómo es el profesor de educación física?
Estricto. Muy estricto con el uniforme.

Descríbeme tu uniforme escolar.
Llevamos unos pantalones negros o una falda negra, una camisa blanca, una chaqueta verde y una corbata de rayas.

¿Crees que el uniforme es una buena idea?
Es una buena idea, pero no es perfecto en mi instituto.

¿Qué cambiarías entonces?
Cambiaría el color de la chaqueta, y las reglas son estrictas.

¿Qué reglas hay en tu instituto?
Muchas.

¿Por ejemplo?
Por ejemplo, el uniforme debe ser perfecto y no se debe comer chicle.

¿Hay actividades extraescolares en tu instituto?
Sí. Ayer fui a un taller de teatro y a veces voy a un club de fotografía.

¿Qué hiciste en el club de fotografía?
–

¿Tienes una pregunta?
–

Marks and commentary

	Communication	Range and accuracy of language	Pronunciation and intonation	Spontaneity and fluency	Total
Marks	5/10	5/10	2/5	3/5	**15/30**

This conversation has been given 5 marks for Communication because the responses are short but with some attempts at narration. Opinions are given and occasionally explained, but they are quite repetitive. A Communication mark is lost because a question has not been asked, despite the teacher-examiner giving a reminder at the end of the conversation.

5 marks are awarded for Range and accuracy of language. Three time frames have been used successfully, even without prompting. Vocabulary is quite limited, however, particularly when giving opinions. Complex linguistic structures are not attempted enough to reach a higher band.

Pronunciation and intonation have been assumed to be quite inconsistent in this instance, and so achieve 2 marks.

For Spontaneity and fluency, it is clear that some pre-learned material has been incorporated but in an appropriate way. Given the low mark for Pronunciation and intonation, it has been assumed that there is hesitation in the delivery at times.

1. In the conversation, highlight any adjectives that have been repeated. What would you replace them with to gain a higher mark for Range and accuracy of language?
2. Complete the conversation successfully by answering the final two questions, the first explaining what you did in photography club and the second by asking the teacher-examiner a question.

Conversation 2: Themes 2 and 3

Y ahora la conversación. Empezamos con el tema dos. ¿Dónde vives exactamente?
Vivo en una ciudad en el noroeste de Inglaterra desde hace ocho años. En el pasado vivía en un pueblo.

¿Cómo era ese pueblo?
No sé exactamente, pero mi madre dice que era pequeño y bastante tranquilo. Tenía una población de mil personas.

¿Cómo es la ciudad donde vives ahora?
Pienso que es bastante grande y a mí me fascina porque es muy cultural. Hay muchos museos y monumentos. Tenemos muchos turistas.

Y ¿qué no te gusta de tu ciudad?
En este momento, está un poco sucia y es peligrosa. Necesita más apoyo e inversión.

¿Por qué es peligrosa? ¿Hay problemas sociales?
Sí, hay varios problemas sociales. Hay violencia callejera a causa del narcotráfico y hay cada vez más personas sin techo. Afortunadamente, por lo general es una ciudad acogedora.

Háblame de tu casa.
Vivo en un piso moderno en el centro de la ciudad. El piso tiene ocho habitaciones. Mi habitación favorita es mi dormitorio porque es cómodo.

¿Qué hay en tu dormitorio?
Hay una cama blanca, una alfombra amarilla y una lámpara elegante. A la derecha del armario hay una estantería que es bastante antigua.

¿Dónde te gustaría vivir en el futuro?
Me gustaría vivir en Londres porque hay muchas oportunidades de trabajo allí. Además, hay mucha diversidad cultural.

¿Cuáles son las desventajas de vivir en Londres?
Es verdad que hay varios problemas sociales y medioambientales en Londres. Primero, hay demasiada contaminación porque la población es enorme y la desigualdad es insoportable.

Cambiamos de tema y ahora es el tema número tres. ¿Qué asignaturas estudias?
En mi instituto estudio ocho asignaturas, pero el año que viene estudiaré solo tres asignaturas.

¿Qué estudiarás el año que viene?
Estudiaré química, física y biología. Serán muy útiles porque quiero ser médico en el futuro.

¿Cómo son los profesores de tu instituto?
En mi opinión, la mayoría son muy simpáticos y comprensivos. El problema es que algunos son muy estrictos. Si tienes muchos deberes, es estresante a veces. Además, hay castigos duros si no llevas el uniforme correctamente.

Descríbeme tu uniforme escolar.
Llevamos unos pantalones negros o una falda negra, una camisa blanca, una chaqueta verde y una corbata de rayas. Solemos llevar un jersey negro.

¿Crees que el uniforme es una buena idea?
Es una buena idea porque fomenta la igualdad. No obstante, personalmente, yo cambiaría el color de la chaqueta. Además, mis padres piensan que cuesta demasiado.

¿Qué reglas hay en tu instituto?
Hay un montón de reglas diferentes. No se debe comer chicle ni insultar a otros estudiantes. Está prohibido correr por los pasillos.

¿Hiciste algunas actividades extraescolares la semana pasada?
Sí, fui a un club de fotografía y a un taller de teatro.

¿Qué hiciste en el club de fotografía?
Me interesa sacar fotos de la naturaleza. Mostré al profesor unas fotos que saqué en un bosque cerca de mi casa. ¿Te gusta la fotografía?

Marks and commentary

	Communication	Range and accuracy of language	Pronunciation and intonation	Spontaneity and fluency	Total
Marks	10/10	10/10	5/5	5/5	**30/30**

This conversation has been given 10 marks for Communication because it is a confident performance with a range of mature opinions. The question asked is acceptable, although waiting until the end of conversation to ask it is risky, especially given that the full answers could make the conversation go over the allocated seven minutes. It improves considerably on the first response, with much greater detail and development.

10 marks are achieved for Range and accuracy of language. The range of vocabulary is exceptional, particularly verbs such as *fomentar* and *soler*. Past and future tenses are used throughout the conversation, as are a range of complex structures: for example, *a mí me fascina* ('it fascinates me') and *hay castigos duros si no…* ('there are harsh punishments if you don't…').

Pronunciation and intonation have been assumed to be consistently good and so 5 marks are awarded.

For Spontaneity and fluency, the full 5 marks are given. The conversation flows naturally, and any pre-learned material is integrated seamlessly into the conversation.

> 1. In the conversation find three examples of:
>   - the imperfect tense
>   - the future tense.
>
> 2. Extend all of the answers that include an imperfect or future tense. Add more verbs in these tenses, along with some ambitious vocabulary.

Please see the AQA GCSE Spanish specification for further details of the assessment criteria:
https://filestore.aqa.org.uk/resources/spanish/specifications/AQA-8698-SP-2016.PDF

Model answers and mark schemes

AQA GCSE Spanish (9–1)

H

Higher Tier Paper 3 Reading

Time allowed: 1 hour

Instructions

- Answer **all** questions.
- Answer the questions in the spaces provided.
- In **Section A**, answer the questions in **English**. In **Section B**, answer the questions in **Spanish**. In **Section C**, translate the passage into **English**.
- Cross through any work you do not want to be marked.

Information

- The marks for the questions are shown in brackets.
- The maximum mark for this paper is 60.
- You must **not** use a dictionary.

Please note: The Practice Paper questions and answers have not been written or approved by AQA.

Section A   Questions and answers in **English**

| 0 | 1 | **Environment**

You are in an Argentinian school with your friend and you see this poster.

USA SOLO LA ENERGÍA QUE NECESITES.

POR FAVOR, APAGA LAS LUCES.

Answer the question in **English**.

Example   What is the poster about?

Saving energy.

| 0 | 1 | . | 1 | What does the poster ask you to do?

[1 mark]

0 2   Education

You are reading an article on your Spanish friend's school website.

Instituto de Enseñanza Secundaria Cumbres Verdes

Cursos de formación profesional

Además de la educación secundaria, nuestro centro ya ofrece una gran variedad de cursos de formación profesional. El año próximo también tenemos la intención de ofrecer una gama de aprendizajes diferentes.

Nuestra prioridad es preparar a nuestros estudiantes para la vida laboral. La mayoría de los estudiantes encontrarán trabajos durante el primer año después de terminar. Ofrecemos cursos de belleza, peluquería, ingeniería, fontanería y jardinería. Los cursos aún disponibles son el de fontanería y el de jardinería. Todos los cursos comenzarán en noviembre y tendrán una duración mínima de seis meses.

In many multiple-choice questions, all of the answers seem possible. This is a deliberate ploy to really test your comprehension skills. Look very carefully at the relevant part of the text and read it over and over until you are sure of the meaning, then try to rule out the other options.

Write the correct letter in each box.

0 2 . 1   According to the website, what does Cumbres Verdes school now offer?

A	Professional training courses.
B	A range of apprenticeships.
C	A new learning centre.

[1 mark]

0 2 . 2   What is the school's priority?

A	Making sure students obtain a year-long placement.
B	Getting students ready for their working life.
C	Encouraging students to work hard.

[1 mark]

0 2 . 3   In what way do the plumbing and gardening courses differ from the others on offer?

A	They start in November.
B	They never last more than six months.
C	They still have places available.

[1 mark]

| 0 | 3 |

A questionnaire on friendships

Your Honduran friend, Óscar, has completed an online questionnaire. Look at the answers he has circled.

> Before you sit your exams, make sure you have access to plenty of reading tasks such as these and perfect your technique. Look at the mark scheme and how much information is needed for each question.

Cómo saber si eres un buen amigo o buena amiga

¿Sabes qué tipo de amigo eres? Haz este test y descubre la verdad.

Example ¿Te gusta pasar tiempo con tus amigos?

(A) Por lo general, prefiero estar solo.
B A veces. Somos un grupo pequeño y leal.
C ¡Un montón! Tenemos mucho en común.

1. Tu mejor amigo te confiesa que tiene un problema personal. ¿Cómo respondes?

A Escucho y le doy consejos.
B N Recomiendo que hable con sus padres.
(C) Le digo que no tengo tiempo para estas cosas.

2. Es tu fiesta de cumpleaños. ¿A quién invitas?

A A toda mi clase del instituto – ¡la popularidad es importante!
(B) Solo a mi familia porque me llevo mejor con ellos.
C A un grupo pequeño de amigos cercanos.

3. Cuando te peleas con tu mejor amigo, ¿qué haces después?

A No le hablo en varios días.
B Mando un mensaje de texto para hablar y solucionarlo.
(C) Siempre espero a recibir un mensaje de perdón de mi amigo.

Answer the questions in **English**.

Example   According to the circled answer, do you think Óscar is sociable?

Tick the correct box.

Yes [ ]   No [✓]

Give a reason for your answer.

He says that in general, he prefers to be alone.

| 0 | 3 | . | 1 | According to the circled answer, do you think Óscar is selfish? Tick the correct box.

Yes ☐   No ☐

Give a reason for your answer.

_____

[1 mark]

| 0 | 3 | . | 2 | According to the circled answer, do you think Óscar has a close relationship with his family? Tick the correct box.

Yes ☐   No ☐

Give a reason for your answer.

_____

[1 mark]

| 0 | 3 | . | 3 | According to the circled answer, do you think Óscar is a very forgiving person? Tick the correct box.

Yes ☐   No ☐

Give a reason for your answer.

_____

[1 mark]

0 4   **Internet addiction**

You read this article in a Spanish newspaper.

Answer the questions in **English**.

> **Adicción a Internet y a las tecnologías**
>
> En los países desarrollados, Internet ha causado una revolución en los últimos veinte años y hoy en día es casi imposible vivir sin él. En años recientes, el número de dispositivos de Internet por hogar está en fuerte aumento. Parece que estamos conectados continuamente.
>
> Desafortunadamente, esta red de información y contenidos esencial causa adicción entre los españoles. La mayoría están conectados todo el día con su móvil o tableta, pero también hay cada vez más que ven la televisión en línea y usan asistentes virtuales y relojes inteligentes.
>
> Según el departamento de psicología de la Universidad Autónoma de Madrid, el 57% de los adultos de más de 30 años se conecta tres horas al día mientras que los mayores de 50 años se conectan una hora. Los estudios hablan de que las generaciones futuras se conectarán más de cuatro horas diarias y tendrán problemas de dependencia.

0 4 . 1   Where **exactly** has the internet caused a revolution in recent years?

_____

[1 mark]

0 4 . 2   According to the text, what has seen a sharp increase in recent years?

_____

[1 mark]

0 4 . 3   As well as mobile phones and tablet computers, which other three internet devices are Spanish people using?

_____

[1 mark]

0 4 . 4   Why is the problem of addiction likely to get worse in the future?

_____

[1 mark]

| 0 | 5 |

***Yerma*, a play by Federico García Lorca**

Read these extracts from the play.

What is he writing about?

Write the correct letters in the boxes.

A	Health
B	Travel
C	Children
D	Silence
E	Nature
F	Food

| 0 | 5 | . | 1 |

Tener un hijo no es tener un ramo de rosas. Hemos de sufrir para verlos crecer.

[1 mark]

| 0 | 5 | . | 2 |

Cómo me gusta el olor del fango rojo que trae el río por el invierno.

[1 mark]

| 0 | 5 | . | 3 |

Si yo estuviera enferma me gustaría que tú me cuidases.

[1 mark]

| 0 | 5 | . | 4 |

¡Que mi boca se quede muda!

[1 mark]

| 0 | 6 | **A magazine article**

Your Spanish friend sends you a link to an online article about a reality TV programme. Read the article and answer the questions that follow in **English**.

Gran Hermano VIP

El tradicional programa de telerrealidad *Gran Hermano* parece no interesar mucho a la audiencia en España, pero el canal de televisión Telecinco tiene la solución para despertar la atención de todos: hacer una versión exclusivamente con famosos que dura menos días que el original.

Pero, ¿son realmente famosos los concursantes? En la edición pasada, había una exjugadora de fútbol profesional, un YouTuber famoso que cuelga videos en Internet, dos presentadores de noticias y algunos modelos. Hay gente que no conoce a estos famosos, pero no importa porque lo imprescindible es la combinación de personalidades diferentes.

En la primera semana ya hubo una pelea entre dos concursantes porque el baño estaba muy sucio, y otros momentos de tensión a la hora de cenar y sobre quién hace las camas. ¿Aburrido? En absoluto. ¡Todo un éxito de crítica y con casi cuatro millones de espectadores!

> Make sure you pay attention to the number of marks available in brackets. Although many questions are worth one mark, occasionally, some are worth two or more.

| 0 | 6 |. | 1 | According to the article, why is this series of *Gran Hermano* different to the previous ones? Give **two** reasons.

1

_____

_____

2

_____

_____

[2 marks]

0 6 . 2 Why does it not matter if the participants are not very famous?

_____

_____

[1 mark]

0 6 . 3 Has the programme been well-received by viewers?

Yes ☐   No ☐

Give **two** reasons.

1

_____

_____

2

_____

_____

[2 marks]

| 0 | 7 |

An animal protection group

You read this advert in a Spanish magazine.

Answer the questions in **English**.

> **PRO OSOS ESPAÑA**
>
> El oso pardo o también oso marrón es un mamífero de entre 200 y 250kg de peso que vive en los bosques y montañas del norte de España. Tristemente, este animal está en peligro de extinción debido a la caza, el cambio climático y, sobre todo, la destrucción de su hábitat.
>
> **Pro Osos España** tiene un centro de cuidado intensivo para osos pardos en una aldea de los Pirineos donde nuestros expertos cuidan de los osos enfermos e intentan proteger su hábitat.
>
> *Si quisieras ayudarnos, visita nuestra página web y hazte miembro.*
>
> *¡Ven a limpiar la naturaleza con nosotros!*

> Many exam questions require you to identify a specific piece of information hidden among lots of detail, such as the 'main reason', the best/worst aspect', etc. This information will often, though not always, come at the end of the paragraph.

| 0 | 7 | . | 1 | What is the **main** reason the brown bear is in danger of extinction in Spain?

_____

[1 mark]

| 0 | 7 | . | 2 | In which **two** ways do the experts of Pro Osos España support the brown bear in the Pyrenees?

1

_____

_____

2

_____

_____

[2 marks]

AQA GCSE Spanish Higher Practice Papers © Oxford University Press 2020. Photocopying prohibited

0 8 **Pasatiempos**

You read this interview in a Chilean magazine featuring Lorena Márquez, a reality TV star.

> – **Lorena, ¿qué sueles hacer en tu tiempo libre?**
> – Las actividades acuáticas me interesan mucho. Actualmente, voy a una piscina cubierta local para nadar. Pronto me uniré al club de polo acuático allí también.
>
> – **¿Practicas otros deportes acuáticos en este momento?**
> – No. Hace cinco años lo que me fascinaba era el submarinismo, pero hoy en día prefiero caminar por la montaña.
>
> – **Lorena, ¿estás en contra de la pesca?**
> – Por supuesto. De pequeña pasaba muchas tardes tranquila a orillas del río Cisnes pescando con mi padre, pero la falta de humanidad de los pescadores ya me parece insoportable.

At which point in time of Lorena's life do the following water sports apply?

Write   **P** for something that happened in the **past**.

   N for something that is happening **now**.

   F for something that is going to happen in the **future**.

Write the correct letter in each box.

> To answer these questions correctly, first, identify any time phrases. Then, separate any tenses into two categories. Here is a reminder of their formation:
> • Present, preterite and imperfect tenses: remove the last two letters of the infinitive and add the correct endings.
> • Future tense and conditional: add the correct endings to the infinitive.

0 8 . 1 Swimming ☐ **[1 mark]**

0 8 . 2 Water polo ☐ **[1 mark]**

0 8 . 3 Scuba diving ☐ **[1 mark]**

0 8 . 4 Fishing ☐ **[1 mark]**

| 0 | 9 | **A letter for Ricardo** |

Read this extract from *La Tía Tula*, a novel by Miguel de Unamuno.

> Mi querido Ricardo:
> No sabes bien qué días tan malos estoy pasando desde que murió la pobre Rosa. No sabes bien con cuánta pena te lo digo, pero no pueden continuar nuestras relaciones; no puedo casarme contigo. Mi hermana me sigue rogando desde el otro mundo que yo no abandone a sus hijos, y puesto que tengo estos hijos a que cuidar, no debo ya casarme. Perdóname, Ricardo, perdónamelo, por Dios, y mira bien por qué lo hago. Me cuesta mucha pena porque sé que me quieres y lo que sufrirás con esto. Tú, que eres bueno, comprenderás mis deberes y los motivos de mi resolución y encontrarás otra mujer que no tenga mis obligaciones sagradas y que te pueda hacer más feliz. Adiós, Ricardo, que seas feliz y hagas felices a otros, y ten por seguro que nunca, nunca te olvidara. Gertrudis

Write the correct letter in each box.

| 0 | 9 | . | 1 | Why is Gertrudis writing to Ricardo? |

A	To tell him Rosa has died.
B	To tell him she can't marry him.
C	To tell him she has had a baby.

[1 mark]

| 0 | 9 | . | 2 | Why does Gertrudis ask for Ricardo's forgiveness? |

A	She knows her decision will make him suffer.
B	He is a good man and she has betrayed him.
C	She refused to help his sister.

[1 mark]

| 0 | 9 | . | 3 | What is Gertrudis's wish? |

A	That she will forget Ricardo.
B	That she will be happy.
C	That Ricardo will find another woman.

[1 mark]

1 0 **Las Fallas de Valencia**

You would like to visit Valencia, in the east of Spain and your friend shows you this article.

> A good cultural knowledge can be very useful in certain reading tasks, but you should avoid writing an answer based on your own knowledge – always refer closely to the text.

Answer the questions in **English**.

Fiestas de Valencia

La fiesta de las Fallas de Valencia esconde mensajes que muchos turistas desconocen. Las fallas son grandes esculturas de cartón cargadas de humor y crítica social, que suelen hablar sobre política, famosos y tradiciones.

Este año hay monumentos falleros sobre el presidente del gobierno, y sobre la cantante Shakira y su esposo Gerard Piqué, el jugador de fútbol. De entre todas las fallas, una de ellas se lleva a un museo de Fallas para recordar ese año, mientras que el resto se queman en las plazas de Valencia. La quema es un símbolo muy especial para terminar el invierno y comenzar la primavera.

1 0 . 1 What are the *fallas*? Mention **two** features.

1

_____

_____

2

_____

_____

[**2 marks**]

1 0 . 2 Why are the *fallas* burned at the end of the festival?

_____

[**1 mark**]

Section B — Questions and answers in **Spanish**

1 1   **Un concierto en un hotel de Benidorm**

Completa el texto usando palabras de la lista.

Escribe la letra correcta en cada casilla.

Cada lunes a las ocho de la noche, vamos a recordar la década dorada de la música española de los ochenta con _____ populares. Para los niños hay juegos al aire _____ hasta las diez y si quieres ver las estrellas, puedes tomar una bebida en el jardín hasta la _____.

[3 marks]

A	madrugada
B	fuera
C	hotel
D	cantante
E	canciones
F	libre
G	doce

1 1 . 1   ☐

1 1 . 2   ☐

1 1 . 3   ☐

1 2   **El transporte**

Ves esta página en una revista ecuatoriana sobre opiniones de los medios de transporte urbanos.

> Me chifla vivir en la ciudad capital, pero a veces estoy muy desorientada aquí y raras veces tengo ganas de montar en taxis porque cuestan mucho dinero. Los autocares urbanos son la opción más válida porque son muy económicos, aunque mi padre prefiere viajar en metro porque afirma que es más seguro.
> **Lucrecia**
>
> Cuando me levanto muy temprano para ir al instituto no es posible ir en bicicleta debido a la oscuridad. Mi madre tiene un coche pequeño y nos lleva a mi hermana y a mí. Normalmente mis amigos van en autobús juntos y se ríen mucho.
> **Adrián**

Completa las frases en **español**.

Ejemplo   A Lucrecia le gusta…

vivir en la ciudad capital.

> This style of question is less common but involves a similar technique to those that require an answer to a question in Spanish. Find the answer in the text by locating an expression with the same meaning as the verb at the end of each unfinished statement.

1 2 . 1   Lucrecia casi nunca quiere…

_____

[1 mark]

1 2 . 2   El padre de Lucrecia recomienda…

_____

[1 mark]

1 2 . 3   Para ir al instituto, Adrián no puede…

_____

[1 mark]

1 2 . 4   Los amigos de Adrián suelen…

_____

[1 mark]

1 3   **Las redes sociales**

Lees este artículo en una revista argentina.

> Hoy en día es evidente que la información escrita y los mensajes son menos importantes en las redes sociales que hace cinco años.
> Cada vez más jóvenes menores de veinticinco años usan redes como Instagram, donde lo más importante es la fotografía y las imágenes, sin escribir nada. Instagram requiere que los usuarios tengan una edad mínima de 13 años para crear una cuenta.
> La famosa frase 'Una imagen vale más que mil palabras' se hace realidad con esta nueva manera de compartir estilos de vida, pero hay peligros: los jóvenes no practican la ortografía en su tiempo libre, cada vez escriben y leen peor.

Escribe la letra correcta en cada casilla.

1 3 . 1   ¿Entre quién es cada vez más popular Instagram?

A	Entre los chicos de veinticinco años.
B	Entre los adolescentes y los jóvenes adultos.
C	Entre los menores de trece años.

[1 mark]

1 3 . 2   ¿Qué crees que significa la frase 'Una imagen vale más que mil palabras'?

A	La realidad es muy extraña.
B	Es preferible escribir con mucho detalle.
C	La mejor manera de entender algo es verlo.

[1 mark]

1 3 . 3   ¿Qué peligro menciona el artículo?

A	El analfabetismo
B	La soledad
C	La depresión

[1 mark]

| 1 | 4 |

El acoso escolar

Mira estos comentarios de dos estudiantes guatemaltecos sobre el acoso escolar.

> When answering questions in Spanish, there is no need to re-phrase or use complex language; concentrate on locating the correct information to answer the question and lift it out of the text. Don't lift out irrelevant information or you won't get the mark!

Omar
No tengo problemas de acoso en mi centro educativo, pero me preocupa que otros estudiantes sufran en silencio, sobre todo los estudiantes más jóvenes. Mi instituto debe crear un grupo de apoyo para las víctimas de acoso.

Marieta
Mi instituto tiene una asociación de estudiantes mayores de dieciséis años que aconsejan a los estudiantes sobre los peligros del acoso. Sin embargo, me gustaría que los profesores también intentasen ayudar a la asociación más a menudo.

Contesta a las preguntas en **español**.

| 1 | 4 | . | 1 | ¿De qué se preocupa Omar?

_____

[1 mark]

| 1 | 4 | . | 2 | ¿Qué recomienda Omar?

_____

[1 mark]

| 1 | 4 | . | 3 | Según Marieta, ¿de qué sirve la asociación de estudiantes mayores?

_____

[1 mark]

| 1 | 4 | . | 4 | ¿Qué podrían hacer los profesores en el instituto de Marieta?

_____

[1 mark]

1 5   **La agenda de Patricia**

Tu amiga Patricia te enseña sus planes.

---

martes 20:30h
Mi tía viene a cenar. ¡Qué rollo! Habla mucho y me fastidia un montón.

miércoles 16:00h
Después del instituto iré a la piscina durante una hora con mi amiga Laura. ¡Qué relajante!

jueves 08:00h
Lo peor de la semana: visita al dentista, me duelen las muelas.

viernes 18:45h
Vamos al cine con los primos Germán y Rodrigo. Veremos una película de miedo.

sábado 22:30h
Día de compras, luego cena en un restaurante en Madrid. ¡Qué divertido!

domingo 13:40h
Veré el tenis en la tele. Juega Rafa Nadal, creo que es un jugador increíble.

lunes 9:00h
¡Una nueva semana en el instituto!
Empiezo con francés, y después educación física.

Contesta a las preguntas en **español**.

Ejemplo   ¿Qué día Patricia vio deportes en casa?

domingo
_____

1 5 . 1   ¿Qué día Patricia comenzó el día con un idioma extranjero?

_____

[1 mark]

1 5 . 2   ¿Qué día Patricia disfrutó de un filme de terror?

_____

[1 mark]

1 5 . 3   ¿Qué día Patricia nadó durante un rato con una compañera?

_____

[1 mark]

1 5 . 4   ¿Qué día Patricia pasó un día entretenido en la capital?

_____

[1 mark]

Section C   Translation into **English**

| 1 | 6 |

You read this item in a local newspaper.

Translate it into **English** for a friend.

> Always try to leave enough time in your exam to read over your answer carefully at the end and check the quality of English.

> Barcelona es una ciudad con mucho turismo. El año pasado recibió más visitas que nunca, y los hoteles estaban casi todos llenos durante la primavera y el verano. 'Lo mejor de la ciudad es su clima y la comida fresca' dice Imelda, una turista irlandesa. 'Ayer mi novio y yo lo pasamos muy bien. Volveremos muy pronto.'

[9 marks]

_____

_____

_____

_____

_____

_____

_____

_____

_____

_____

_____

_____

END OF QUESTIONS

Model answers and mark schemes

AQA GCSE Spanish (9–1)

Higher Tier Paper 4 Writing

Time allowed: 1 hour 15 minutes

Instructions
- You must answer **three** questions.
- You must answer **either** Question 1.1 **or** Question 1.2. Do not answer both of these questions.
- You must answer **either** Question 2.1 **or** Question 2.2. Do not answer both of these questions.
- You must answer Question 3.
- Answer **all** questions in **Spanish**.
- Answer the questions in the spaces provided.
- Cross through any work you do not want to be marked.

Information
- The marks for the questions are shown in brackets.
- The maximum mark for this paper is 60.
- You must **not** use a dictionary during this test.
- In order to score the highest marks for Question 1.1/Question 1.2, you must write something about each bullet point. You must use a variety of vocabulary and structures and include your opinions.
- In order to score the highest marks for Question 2.1/Question 2.2, you must write something about both bullet points. You must use a variety of vocabulary and structures and include your opinions and reasons.

Please note: The Practice Paper questions and answers have not been written or approved by AQA.

Answer **either** Question 1.1 **or** Question 1.2.
You must **not** answer **both** of these questions.

EITHER Question 1.1

| 0 | 1 | . | 1 |

Escribes un blog para un colegio español sobre el uso de Internet en tu país.

Menciona:

- cómo usaste Internet el fin de semana pasado
- tu opinión sobre los peligros de Internet
- cómo vas a usar Internet para preparar tus próximos exámenes
- tu aparato electrónico favorito.

Escribe aproximadamente **90** palabras en **español**.
Responde a todos los aspectos de la pregunta.

[16 marks]

OR Question 1.2

| 0 | 1 | . | 2 |

Tu amigo ecuatoriano te manda un email y te pregunta sobre tu instituto.

Responde a su email.

Menciona:

- qué hiciste en el instituto el viernes pasado
- tu opinión sobre las instalaciones
- qué asignaturas te gustan más
- qué vas a hacer el año que viene.

Escribe aproximadamente **90** palabras en **español**.
Responde a todos los aspectos de la pregunta.

[16 marks]

- Identify which time frames you need for each bullet and check that your tenses are accurate. The first bullet contains the preterite *usaste*, so you need to refer to the past when answering; the third bullet contains the near future *vas a usar*, so there needs to be a reference to the future.
- You can use the language of the bullet points to help structure your response, particularly when you are unsure.

- To attain the highest marks in Question 1 of the Higher Writing paper, you must cover all four bullet points (although not necessarily equally), use a wide range of relevant topic-specific vocabulary and express at least two opinions, avoiding obvious repetition.
- Remember to justify your opinions with reasons as much as possible: *me gustan mucho las matemáticas porque son útiles y la profesora es divertida*. Include connectives to create longer sentences, such as *por un lado… y por otro…, además*.
- You will need to refer to all three time frames in your answer (past, present and future), so check that your verb tenses are accurate.

Answer **either** Question 2.1 **or** Question 2.2.
You must **not** answer **both** of these questions.

EITHER Question 2.1

| 0 | 2 | . | 1 | Tu revista en línea favorita te invita a escribir un artículo con el título 'Verano de vacaciones'.

Decides participar con esta información:

• las ventajas y desventajas de viajar en verano

• qué vas a hacer en el futuro para tener un verano inolvidable.

Escribe aproximadamente **150** palabras en **español**. Responde a los dos aspectos de la pregunta.

[32 marks]

• Question 2 always contains two bullet points. While you must cover both bullet points in reasonable detail, there is no need for equal coverage, but you do need to make sure that your answers to each point are fully relevant.
• In the first bullet, you need to write about both the advantages and disadvantages of travelling in summer, consider using connectives and phrases to communicate the two sides of an argument.
• Notice that the second bullet targets the future time frame, so use one or more future tenses (*voy a viajar, viajaré, viajaría* etc.) in your answer.
• You can use the language of the bullet point to help you respond. For example, for the second bullet point you could start your response: *En el futuro, para tener un verano inolvidable, voy a viajar…*

OR Question 2.2

| 0 | 2 | . | 2 | Lees un blog con el título 'Lo mejor y lo peor de los trabajos para adolescentes'.

Decides escribir un comentario en el blog con esta información:

• qué trabajos has hecho para ganar dinero

• tus opiniones sobre trabajar a los dieciséis años.

Escribe aproximadamente **150** palabras en **español**. Responde a los dos aspectos de la pregunta.

[32 marks]

• You are allowed to write more than the recommended word count, but doing so often leads to more language errors and repetition of key points.
• In the first bullet, you need to write about more than one job (*trabajos*) that you have done in the past; it will not be enough to focus on just one job as you won't gain as many marks. Use past time markers such as *primero, luego, después,* to help structure your response.
• Remember the rule – simple and clear is better than complex and unclear. Stick to what you know and try to avoid being overambitious with your sentences.

| 0 | 3 |

Translate the following passage into **Spanish**.

> I don't like swimming in my school because the water is cold and the new swimming pool is not clean. Last week, however, I played basketball and tomorrow I am going to play in a local competition. I get on well with my friends and we are going to win. Tonight I have to sleep well.

[12 marks]

- As you translate, make sure you do not miss out any parts of the text by accident. Doing so can cost you valuable marks!
- High-frequency words and phrases will come up regularly, so be prepared: examples include, connectives (*pero, y, o, porque, luego, entonces, sin embargo, también, aunque, además* etc.).
- It pays to check and double-check your verb tenses and endings carefully as you translate. Getting these wrong can mean that you have not conveyed key messages nor applied grammatical knowledge correctly.
- If one of the key messages contains a minor error or errors, it will still be credited, but an accumulation of minor errors will have a negative effect on your overall mark for the application of grammatical knowledge.

END OF QUESTIONS

Model answers and mark schemes

AQA GCSE Spanish (9–1)

H

Higher Tier Paper 1 Listening

Time allowed: 45 minutes
(including 5 minutes' reading time before the test)

You will need no other materials.
The pauses are pre-recorded for this test.

Information
- The marks for the questions are shown in brackets. The maximum mark for this paper is 50.
- You must **not** use a dictionary.

Advice
This is what you should do for each item.
- After the question number is announced, there will be a pause to allow you to read the instructions and questions.
- Listen carefully to the recording and read the questions again.
- Listen to the recording again, and then answer the questions.
- When the next question is about to start you will hear a bleep.
- You may write at any time during the test.
- In **Section A**, answer the questions in **English**. In **Section B**, answer the questions in **Spanish**.
- You must answer all the questions in the spaces provided. Do not write on blank pages.
- Write neatly and put down all the information you are asked to give.
- **You must not ask questions or interrupt during the test.**
- You have five minutes to read through the question paper. You may make notes during this time. You may turn to the questions now.
- **The test starts now.**

Listen to the audio

Please note: The Practice Paper questions and answers have not been written or approved by AQA.

Section A   Questions and answers in **English**

0 1   **A gap year**

Your friend from El Salvador, Elías, is talking to his teacher about plans for after the exams.

You listen to the conversation.

Answer **both** parts of the question in **English**.

0 1 . 1   What does Elías intend to do on his gap year?

_____

[1 mark]

0 1 . 2   What is his teacher's recommendation?

_____

[1 mark]

Advertisements

While listening to a Spanish local radio station, you hear some advertisements.

A	Shampoo
B	Holiday apartments
C	Make-up
D	TV series
E	Healthy drink
F	Smart watch
G	Home insurance

Match the correct summary to each advertisement.

Write the correct letter in each box.

| 0 | 2 | | [1 mark] |

| 0 | 3 | | [1 mark] |

| 0 | 4 | | [1 mark] |

| 0 | 5 | | [1 mark] |

| 0 | 6 | | [1 mark] |

| 0 | 7 | **A debate about bullfighting** |

You are listening to a podcast on Spanish radio about bullfighting.

What is each person's opinion?

Write   **P** for a positive opinion.

   N for a negative opinion.

   P+N for a **positive** and **negative** opinion.

| 0 | 7 | . | 1 | **Adela** | | [1 mark] |

| 0 | 7 | . | 2 | **Iker** | | [1 mark] |

| 0 | 7 | . | 3 | **Lola** | | [1 mark] |

| 0 | 7 | . | 4 | **Hasan** | | [1 mark] |

Family conflict

You are listening to a radio phone-in in which callers are talking about conflict within their families.

For each speaker, which statements are correct?

Write   **A** if only statement **A** is **correct**.

        B if only statement **B** is **correct**.

        A+B if both statements **A** and **B** are **correct**.

0	8

A	She always argues with all of her siblings.
B	Her elder sister never lets her use her tablet computer.

Write the correct letter(s) in the box.   **[1 mark]**

0	9

A	The relationship with his stepmother has got worse.
B	He is trying to adopt a more mature attitude towards family life.

Write the correct letter(s) in the box.   **[1 mark]**

1	0

A	Her husband would like to divorce her quickly.
B	She and her husband do not have children, so a divorce would not be difficult.

Write the correct letter(s) in the box.   **[1 mark]**

1	1

A	She can't bear the fact that her parents do not let her stay out late.
B	She believes that the best option would be to move out as soon as possible.

Write the correct letter(s) in the box.   **[1 mark]**

An interview with Paula Valero

You are watching a video interview with Spanish online celebrity, Paula Valero.

Answer **both** parts of the question in **English**.

| 1 | 2 | . | 1 | What is the hardest aspect of Paula's job?

_____

[1 mark]

| 1 | 2 | . | 2 | What also annoys her?

_____

[1 mark]

Answer **both** parts of the question in **English**.

| 1 | 3 | . | 1 | Why is Paula celebrating?

_____

[1 mark]

| 1 | 3 | . | 2 | What is another advantage of her job?

_____

[1 mark]

University degrees

You hear two advertisements for the University of Huelva.

Answer in **English**.

| 1 | 4 |

Explain why you should study maths or sciences at the University of Huelva.

_____

[1 mark]

Answer **both** parts of the question in **English**.

| 1 | 5 |

What are the **two** advantages of the plumbing and electrician courses?

1

_____

_____

2

_____

_____

[2 marks]

TV on demand

While in Spain, you are listening to your Spanish friends discuss what to watch on television.

For each speaker, choose the type of TV programme and write the correct letter in the box.

Why do they recommend each programme? Answer in **English**.

A	Music
B	Sports
C	Cookery
D	News
E	Quiz
F	Reality

Example

Programme	Recommended because...
A	*It's the most popular programme in Spain.*

1 6

[ ]

_____

[2 marks]

1 7

[ ]

_____

[2 marks]

1 8

[ ]

_____

[2 marks]

An environmental report

You are watching a documentary about the Spanish city of Cartagena and its environmental problems.

Answer **both** parts of the question in **English**.

| 1 | 9 | . | 1 | Why is the Mar Menor lagoon under threat?

_____

[1 mark]

| 1 | 9 | . | 2 | Why might the economy of Cartagena suffer?

_____

[1 mark]

The documentary continues.

Answers **both** parts of the question in **English**.

| 2 | 0 | . | 1 | What are the locals planning to do?

_____

[1 mark]

| 2 | 0 | . | 2 | What has the government proposed?

_____

[1 mark]

Interview with Spanish singer, Rosa

You are watching a Spanish TV programme in which Rosa is being interviewed about her career.

What questions does the interviewer ask her?

Answer in **English**.

Example   Are you happy with the success of your latest video?

2 1

_____

_____

[1 mark]

2 2

_____

_____

[1 mark]

2 3

_____

_____

[1 mark]

School subjects

Your Colombian friends, María and Pancho, talking about their school subjects.

What is their opinion of these subjects?

Write   **P** for a **positive** opinion.

  N for a **negative** opinion.

  P+N for a **positive** and **negative** opinion.

2 4   María

La educación física ☐   La historia ☐   **[2 marks]**

2 5   Pancho

El dibujo ☐   Las matemáticas ☐   **[2 marks]**

Section B   Questions and answers in **Spanish**

Los pasatiempos

Escuchas unas entrevistas en la radio española.

¿De qué pasatiempos hablan las personas y cuándo?

Completa la tabla en **español**.

Ejemplo   Nina

Pasatiempo en el pasado	Pasatiempo ahora	Ambición para el futuro
(el) atletismo	*baile*	*ser bailarina profesional*

2	6

Fausto

Pasatiempo en el pasado	Pasatiempo ahora	Ambición para el futuro
		escalar las montañas

[2 marks]

2	7

Marta

Pasatiempo en el pasado	Pasatiempo ahora	Ambición para el futuro
	el judo	

[2 marks]

En la ciudad

Escuchas a unos amigos hablar de los sitios que visitan en la ciudad.

Indica de qué sitio habla exactamente cada persona.

Contesta en **español**.

Ejemplo   (el) estadio

2 8

_____

[1 mark]

2 9

_____

[1 mark]

3 0

_____

[1 mark]

| 3 | 1 | **Jorge y las reglas del instituto**

Tu amigo español, Jorge, te cuenta cosas sobre su instituto.

Contesta en **español**.

| 3 | 1 |.| 1 | ¿Qué es interesante sobre el instituto de Jorge?

_____

[1 mark]

| 3 | 1 |.| 2 | ¿Cuál es la ventaja y la desventaja de estudiar allí?

A	el horario
B	las reglas
C	el menú
D	la localización
E	las asignaturas

Escribe la letra correcta en cada casilla.

Ventaja

Desventaja   **[2 marks]**

END OF QUESTIONS

Answers and mark schemes

AQA GCSE Spanish (9–1)

Higher Tier Paper 2 Speaking

Time allowed: 10–12 minutes
(+12 minutes' supervised preparation time)

Candidate's material – Role-play and Photo card

Instructions

- During the preparation time you must prepare the Role-play card and Photo card given to you.
- You may make notes during the preparation time on the paper provided by your teacher-examiner. Do not write on the stimulus cards.
- Hand your notes and both stimulus cards to the teacher-examiner before the General Conversation.
- You must ask the teacher-examiner at least one question in the General Conversation.

Information

- The test will last a maximum of 12 minutes and will consist of a Role-play (approximately 2 minutes) and a Photo card (approximately 3 minutes), followed by a General Conversation (between 5 and 7 minutes) based on your nominated Theme and the remaining Theme which has not been covered in the Photo card.
- You must **not** use a dictionary at any time during the test. This includes the preparation time.

Teacher Part

Please note: The Practice Paper questions and answers have not been written or approved by AQA.

ROLE-PLAY 1

CANDIDATE'S ROLE

Part 1

Instructions to candidates

Your teacher will play the part of your Mexican friend and will speak first.

You should address your friend as *tú*.

When you see this – **!** – you will have to respond to something you have not prepared.

When you see this – **?** – you will have to ask a question.

Estás hablando con tu amigo mexicano / tu amiga mexicana sobre el matrimonio.

- Tu novio/novia ideal – cualidades (**dos** detalles)
- **!**
- Tu opinión sobre la ceremonia de la boda (**dos** detalles)
- **?** El matrimonio – opinión
- Una causa de divorcios

ROLE-PLAY 2

CANDIDATE'S ROLE

Part 1

Instructions to candidates

Your teacher will play the part of your Peruvian friend and will speak first.

You should address your friend as *tú*.

When you see this – **!** – you will have to respond to something you have not prepared.

When you see this – **?** – you will have to ask a question.

Estás hablando con tu amigo peruano / tu amiga peruana sobre la dieta.

- Tu comida favorita – razón

- La comida rápida – **un** aspecto positivo y **un** aspecto negativo

- La última vez que fuiste a un restaurante (**dos** detalles)

- **!**

- **?** deporte solo o con amigos

ROLE-PLAY 3

CANDIDATE'S ROLE

Part 1

Instructions to candidates

Your teacher will play the part of a student selling tickets for a theatre production showing at a Spanish university.

You should address the student as *tú*.

When you see this – **!** – you will have to respond to something you have not prepared.

When you see this – **?** – you will have to ask a question.

Estás hablando con un estudiante / una estudiante en una universidad española.

- Entradas – cuántas

- Sesión – cuándo y con quién

- **?** Obra de teatro

- **!**

- Planes para estudiar el año que viene (**dos** detalles)

Card A

Part 2

Candidate's Photo card

- Look at the photo during the preparation period.

- Make any notes you wish to on an additional piece of paper.

- Your teacher will then ask you questions about the photo and about topics related to **global issues**.

Your teacher will ask you the following three questions and then **two more questions** which you have not prepared.

- ¿Qué hay en la foto?

- ¿Qué alternativas hay para las personas en esta situación?

- ¿Cómo se podría terminar con este problema social?

Card B

Part 2

Candidate's Photo card

- Look at the photo during the preparation period.

- Make any notes you wish to on an additional piece of paper.

- Your teacher will then ask you questions about the photo and about topics related to **life at school/college**.

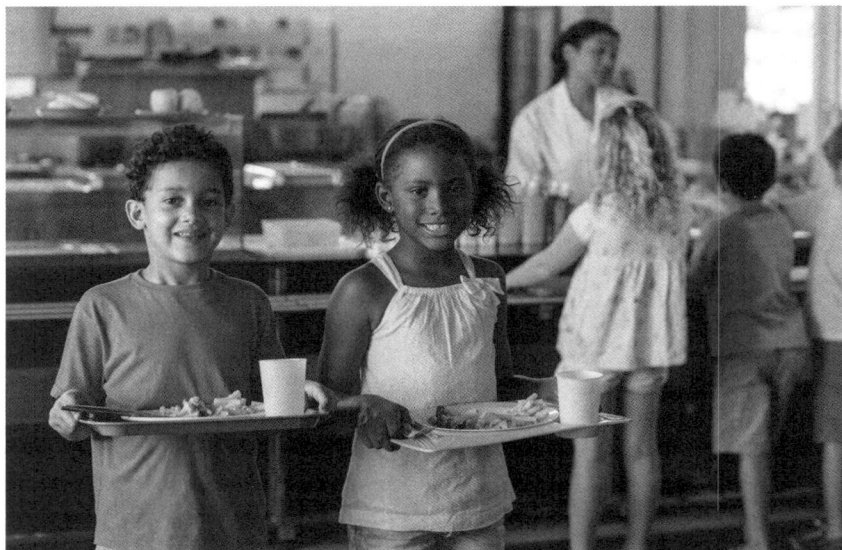

Your teacher will ask you the following three questions and then **two more questions** which you have not prepared.

- ¿Qué hay en la foto?

- ¿Crees que las reglas estrictas de un instituto ayudan a la educación?… ¿Por qué (no)?

- ¿Cómo han cambiado las instalaciones de tu instituto en años recientes?

Card C

Part 2

Candidate's Photo card

- Look at the photo during the preparation period.

- Make any notes you wish to on an additional piece of paper.

- Your teacher will then ask you questions about the photo and about topics related to **free-time activities**.

Your teacher will ask you the following three questions and then **two more questions** which you have not prepared.

- ¿Qué hay en la foto?

- En tu opinión, ¿se debe prohibir esta tradición?

- ¿A qué otros festivales hispanos te gustaría ir?

GENERAL CONVERSATION

Part 3

The Photo card is followed by a General Conversation. The first part of the conversation will be on a theme nominated by the candidate and the second part on the other theme not covered by the Photo card. The total time for the General Conversation will be between 5 and 7 minutes and a similar amount of time should be spent on each theme. Here is a reminder of the three themes:

- Identity and culture
- Local, national, international and global areas of interest
- Current and future study and employment

The following pages show two examples of the general conversation with accompanying commentary on how these conversations would be marked, followed by tasks.

Conversation 1: Themes 1 and 3

Y ahora la conversación. Empezamos con el tema uno. ¿Qué haces en tu tiempo libre?
En mi tiempo libre me gusta jugar al baloncesto.

¿Por qué te gusta el baloncesto?
Me gusta mucho.

¿Hay algún deporte que no te guste?
Sí, el golf es un poco aburrido.

¿Qué actividades hiciste el fin de semana pasado?
El fin de semana pasado fui al cine.

Describe tu visita al cine.
Fui con mis amigos. Me gusta mucho el cine.

¿Por qué te gusta el cine?
El cine es divertido.

¿Cuál es tu película favorita?
Me gustan las películas de ciencia ficción.

¿Qué otros pasatiempos tienes?
–

¿Te gusta leer?
No.

¿Por qué?
Es aburrido.

¿Prefieres ver la televisión?
No veo la tele, pero me gusta navegar por Internet.

¿Qué aplicaciones usas?
En mi móvil, uso Twitter porque es posible leer las noticias rápidamente y es divertido.

¿Qué es lo malo de las redes sociales?
A veces hay personas que sufren acoso.

¿Usas otras aplicaciones?
Sí, uso Tik Tok de vez en cuando. Es divertido si te gusta la música o si te gusta bailar.

Cambiamos de tema y ahora es el tema tres. ¿Tienes un trabajo a tiempo parcial?
Sí, trabajo de canguro.

¿Qué haces exactamente?
Mis primos tienen cinco y ocho años. Trabajo de canguro.

¿Qué haces cuando trabajas de canguro?
–

¿Es un trabajo difícil?
No, porque los hijos son muy simpáticos.

¿Ganas mucho dinero?
Gano veinte euros al mes.

¿Qué trabajo te gustaría hacer en el futuro?
Me gustaría trabajar de abogado.

¿Por qué te gustaría ser abogado?
El salario es muy bueno, pero es difícil a veces. Estudio mucho en mi instituto.

¿Cómo eres laboralmente?
Soy entusiasta y trabajador.

Describe tus prácticas laborales del año pasado.
Trabajé en una oficina.

¿Qué hiciste?
–

¿Qué planes futuros tienes después de los exámenes?
Voy a ir de vacaciones con mis amigos.

Marks and commentary

	Communication	Range and accuracy of language	Pronunciation and intonation	Spontaneity and fluency	Total
Marks	4/10	5/10	2/5	3/5	**14/30**

This conversation has been given 4 marks for Communication because there is a lot of repetition of vocabulary, particularly opinions. There are also only some successful attempts at extending responses in sufficient detail, creating a limited conversation overall. No question is asked of the teacher-examiner which results in a deduction of 1 mark.

5 marks are awarded for Range and accuracy of language. Three time frames have been used correctly on several occasions, although there is a lack of complex structures and ambitious vocabulary. Answers generally contain either a simple opinion expression or verb and fact. There is little variety or attempt to extend sentences required for the next level up.

Pronunciation and intonation have been assumed to be generally fine and gain 2 marks.

For Spontaneity and fluency, it is a basic but generally good exchange with the teacher-examiner. There is evidence of natural reaction to the questions asked, and even if some of the material is pre-learned (particularly in relation to social media), it is used in the right place. 3 marks are therefore given.

> 1. In the conversation, the expression *me gusta* is used five times. Improve the response by changing this expression each time it appears for a different one that carries a similar meaning.
> 2. Improve the answer relating to the office work experience by adding details such as working hours, pay, specific tasks in the role and an opinion. Write your answer in the preterite tense.

Conversation 2: Themes 1 and 3

Y ahora la conversación. Empezamos con el tema uno. ¿Qué haces en tu tiempo libre?
En mi tiempo libre suelo jugar al baloncesto. Lo juego desde hace seis años. Una ventaja es que soy bastante alto y fuerte. Lo malo es que sufrí una lesión el mes pasado.

¿Qué pasó?
Durante un partido me caí y me torcí el tobillo. ¡Qué desastre!

Entonces, ¿no juegas al baloncesto actualmente?
No, no puedo. Juego a los videojuegos en casa. Es mi pasatiempo favorito.

¿Por qué te gustan los videojuegos?
Son entretenidos y además es una manera de evitar el estrés. Me relajo con mis amigos o juego en línea. Tengo una conexión inalámbrica muy rápida.

¿Qué piensas de Internet?
Pienso que es muy útil. Hay algunos peligros, pero muchísimos beneficios. Por ejemplo, se puede jugar a los videojuegos en línea, buscar información rápidamente, ir de compras… ¡Es esencial!

¿Cuáles son los peligros?
Es muy adictivo y a veces es una pérdida de tiempo, sobre todo si ves videos en YouTube o si usas aplicaciones como Facebook o Instagram.

¿Qué vas a hacer este fin de semana?

Primero, voy a levantarme bastante tarde. Luego, voy a desayunar cereales. Voy a jugar a los videojuegos durante el día y por la noche, voy a cenar en un restaurante con mi familia porque es el cumpleaños de mi padre.

¿Qué vas a cenar en el restaurante?

Es un restaurante español. Voy a pedir una paella vegetariana.

¿Crees que tienes una dieta sana?

Claro que sí. No como ni carne ni dulces y solo bebo agua. Hago mucho ejercicio también.

Cambiamos de tema y ahora es el tema tres. ¿Tienes un trabajo a tiempo parcial?

Sí, trabajo de canguro de vez en cuando. No me interesa mucho, pero me pagan bastante bien y no es difícil.

¿Qué haces exactamente?

Mis primos son gemelos. Tienen ocho años y son muy simpáticos. Se comportan muy bien y siempre me escuchan. Juego un poco con ellos, luego se acuestan a las diez. Después, veo la tele un poco.

¿Qué trabajo te gustaría hacer en el futuro?

Me gustaría trabajar de abogado.

¿Por qué te gustaría ser abogado?

Es un trabajo que me fascina desde hace mucho tiempo. Además, el salario es muy bueno. Es verdad que puede ser exigente, pero vale la pena.

¿Cómo eres laboralmente?

Creo que soy entusiasta y trabajador. Estudio mucho y siempre hago los deberes. A veces soy un poco tímido, pero soy joven. Y tú, ¿cómo eres?

Soy bastante inteligente y amable. Describe tus prácticas laborales del año pasado.

Trabajé en una escuela primaria cerca de mi casa. Tuve que ayudar a los profesores, leer libros con los estudiantes, hacer fotocopias…

¿Cómo fue la experiencia?

Fue una experiencia positiva por lo general. Aprendí muchas habilidades sociales.

¿Qué planes futuros tienes después de estos exámenes?

Primero voy a ir de vacaciones con mis amigos, luego quiero seguir con mis estudios aquí.

¿Qué quieres estudiar?

Me apasionan los idiomas y la historia.

¿Qué piensas de tu instituto?

Es ideal para mí. Vivo bastante cerca de aquí, los profesores son buenos y las instalaciones son bastante modernas.

Marks and commentary

	Communication	Range and accuracy of language	Pronunciation and intonation	Spontaneity and fluency	Total
Marks	10/10	10/10	5/5	5/5	**30/30**

This conversation has been given 10 marks for Communication. There is much more narration than in the first response, as demonstrated in the description of a part-time job. Opinions are also more wide-ranging, with a lot of information conveyed. The teacher-examiner speaks much less in this conversation.

10 marks are awarded for Range and accuracy of language. There is a wide variety of more complex linguistic structures, such as *es verdad que* ('it is true that') and *por ejemplo, se puede* ('for example, you can'). There is also extensive use of verbs in past and future tenses. The range of vocabulary is also much more ambitious than in the first response.

Pronunciation and intonation have been assumed to be of a very high standard, reflecting the level of language used. They gain 5 marks.

For Spontaneity and fluency, it is clear that it is a very sophisticated exchange with the teacher-examiner and so it achieves the full 5 marks.

Please see the AQA GCSE Spanish specification for further details of the assessment criteria:
https://filestore.aqa.org.uk/resources/spanish/specifications/AQA-8698-SP-2016.PDF

1. Find the following expressions in the conversation:
   - I usually play
   - it is a way of
   - above all if
   - of course
   - it is worth it
   - I want to continue
   - I am passionate about

2. Now, create a sentence about either your free-time activities or future plans using at least four of these expressions.

Model answers and mark schemes

AQA GCSE Spanish (9–1)

H

Higher Tier Paper 3 Reading

Time allowed: 1 hour

Instructions

- Answer **all** questions.
- Answer the questions in the spaces provided.
- In **Section A**, answer the questions in **English**. In **Section B**, answer the questions in **Spanish**. In **Section C**, translate the passage into **English**.
- Cross through any work you do not want to be marked.

Information

- The marks for the questions are shown in brackets.
- The maximum mark for this paper is 60.
- You must **not** use a dictionary.

Please note: The Practice Paper questions and answers have not been written or approved by AQA.

Section A   Questions and answers in **English**

| 0 | 1 |

Pets in Spain

You read this article about pets in a Spanish magazine.

> **España, el país amante de las mascotas**
> Los amantes de las mascotas son más numerosos en España que hace diez años. La mayoría de los 13 millones de mascotas registradas no vive en el campo, sino en las ciudades. Un estudio reciente afirma que la soledad de la vida ciudadana de hoy en día es la causa principal de ese aumento.
> En Gijón, las mascotas ya están integradas en la vida cotidiana y hay cada vez más áreas verdes donde puedes pasear con el perro suelto. Lorenzo, un gijonés que vive con su perro en un piso de un dormitorio, dice que no le importa el alto coste mensual de mantener su perro porque no podría vivir sin él. Sin embargo, no siempre fue así. Cuando Lorenzo era pequeño, el dueño del apartamento de la familia no le permitía tener animales en casa.

Which **three** statements are true?

Write the correct letters in the boxes.

A	10 years ago, there were fewer pet lovers in Spain.
B	Most pet owners in Spain live in the countryside.
C	Loneliness is now the main reason for pet ownership in cities.
D	In Gijón, dogs must be on leads at all times.
E	Lorenzo is not worried about the high cost of dog ownership.
F	Lorenzo's family did not allow him to have a pet when he was little.

[3 marks]

| 0 | 2 |

Sport

You are reading an interview with Isidora, a Chilean sprinter, in an online newspaper.

> – **Isidora, ¿cuál ha sido el momento más memorable de tu carrera?**
> – Hasta ahora, está claro que cuando llevé la bandera de Chile en la ceremonia de los juegos Pan Americanos, fue muy emocionante e inolvidable.
> – **¿Cuál es tu objetivo este año?**
> – Entreno todos los días para poder ir a los juegos Olímpicos el año que viene. Competí muy bien en las pruebas nacionales hace tres meses, pero la competición olímpica será complicada. Las corredoras de Italia y Alemania son las favoritas.
> – **¿Participarás en otras competiciones?**
> – Quiero dedicarme totalmente en exclusiva a las Olimpiadas, quiero que Chile esté orgulloso de mí.

When does each event take place?

Write   **P** for something that happened in the **past**.

N for something that is happening **now**.

F for something that is going to happen in the **future**.

Write the correct letter in each box.

| 0 | 2 | . | 1 | Carrying the Chilean flag   [1 mark]

| 0 | 2 | . | 2 | Training   [1 mark]

| 0 | 2 | . | 3 | National trials   [1 mark]

| 0 | 2 | . | 4 | Olympic games   [1 mark]

0 3 **A questionnaire on family life**

Your Mexican friend, Hugo, has filled in an online survey. Look at the answers he has circled.

¿Tienes una buena vida familiar?
Haz este test y descubre qué tipo de vida familiar tienes.
Example ¿Pasas tiempo con tu familia los fines de semana?

(A) Mucho
B Un poco
C Nada

1. ¿Crees que riñes con tus padres?

A Nunca
B Lo normal
(C) Raras veces

2. ¿Discutes con tus hermanos sobre qué ver en la televisión?

(A) A menudo
B No mucho
C Jamás

3. ¿Pides perdón después de discutir con tus padres?

A Siempre
(B) ¡Claro que no!
C De vez en cuando

4. ¿Qué tipo de madre o padre serías?

(A) Comprensivo y paciente
B Divertido y gracioso
C Serio y estricto

Example According to the circled answer, how do you know Hugo is close to his family?

  He spends a lot of time with them at the weekend.

Answer the questions in **English**.

0 3 . 1 According to the circled answer, how do you know Hugo gets along with his parents?

_____

_____

[1 mark]

0 3 . 2 According to the circled answer, how do you know Hugo doesn't always get along with his siblings?

_____

_____

[1 mark]

 AQA GCSE Spanish Higher Practice Papers © Oxford University Press 2020. Photocopying prohibited

0 3 . 3 According to the circled answer, how do you know Hugo is a stubborn person?

_____

_____

[1 mark]

0 3 . 4 According to the circled answer, how do you know Hugo would make a good parent?

_____

_____

[1 mark]

| 0 | 4 | **Rural tourism** |

You read this article in a Spanish travel magazine.

Los turistas buscan cada vez más la vida rural

La costa es el destino más popular entre los turistas en España, pero el turismo rural está en aumento. Clara Gil opina que la costa está pasada de moda y es poco entretenida hoy en día ya que no ofrece tantas posibilidades como otros destinos.

Clara prefiere los pueblos rurales desconocidos a los más famosos porque esconden muchos más encantos de los que se cree. Aunque a veces hay una falta de edificios con valor arquitectónico, es innegable que hay maravillas naturales que ofrecen al visitante la posibilidad de pasear por espacios impresionantes.

El año que viene Clara va a volver a la Sierra de Cazorla en Jaén y alojarse en una cabaña de madera tradicional cerca de un valle. Tiene ganas de probar la comida tradicional y, sobre todo, pasear por los bosques nevados.

Write the correct letter in each box.

| 0 | 4 | . | 1 | How does Clara Gil describe coastal holidays nowadays? |

A	Quite entertaining and fashionable.
B	Old-fashioned and not very entertaining.
C	Entertaining with lots of possibilities.

[1 mark]

| 0 | 4 | . | 2 | What type of rural town does Clara prefer to visit? |

A	Those which are least well-known.
B	Those which are famous.
C	Those which are charming.

[1 mark]

| 0 | 4 | . | 3 | According to Clara, what do rural towns offer the visitor? |

A	Breathtaking walks.
B	Architectural beauty.
C	Peace and tranquillity.

[1 mark]

| 0 | 4 | . | 4 | What is Clara most looking forward to doing in Sierra de Cazorla? |

A	Staying in a traditional log cabin.
B	Trying the local food.
C	Walking through the snowy forests.

[1 mark]

0 5   *Juegos de la edad tardía*, a novel by Luis Landero

Read this extract and answer the questions in **English**.

> Gregorio y Angelina habían hecho un viaje a la costa el primer año. Durante el trayecto en tren, enlazaron las manos. Recogieron conchas en la playa y navegaron en una motora. Hablaban de cómo serían felices porque no había ningún motivo que les impidiera no serlo. Gregorio quería tener dos hijos. «No sé», decía Angelina. «Los niños crecen y luego se van».

0 5 . 1   What were Gregorio and Angelina doing during the train journey?

_____

_____

[1 mark]

0 5 . 2   What **two** activities did they do at the coast?

1

_____

_____

2

_____

_____

[2 marks]

0 5 . 3   Why is Angelina unsure about having children?

_____

_____

[1 mark]

| 0 | 6 |

Travel delays

While in Santiago de Chile, you read this sign.

> **ATENCIÓN AL CLIENTE**
>
> Durante el periodo de huelga, el número de vuelos se reducirá a un 33%.
>
> Los viajeros con billetes adquiridos con antelación a los que les haya afectado la huelga, pueden solicitar un reembolso sin coste adicional.

Answer the questions in **English**.

| 0 | 6 | . | 1 | What building are you in?

_____

[1 mark]

| 0 | 6 | . | 2 | What has caused the inconvenience?

_____

[1 mark]

| 0 | 6 | . | 3 | What can people do if they are affected?

_____

[1 mark]

AQA GCSE Spanish Higher Practice Papers © Oxford University Press 2020. Photocopying prohibited

0	7

Healthy living

You come across this article on a news website.

> **Los beneficios de la dieta mediterránea**
>
> En España, parece que tienen el secreto para una vida larga: la dieta mediterránea. Rica en vitaminas, minerales y proteínas, los expertos nutricionistas afirman que lo mejor de esta dieta es la variedad de alimentos frescos.
>
> A pesar de la subida de los precios en los supermercados españoles, los españoles todavía son los europeos que más pescado y carne fresca consumen al año. Los beneficios para la salud que supone esta dieta son más significativos cuando se combinan con el ejercicio físico diario. Se recomienda al menos 30 minutos diarios, cinco días por semana.

Answer the questions in **English**.

0 7 . 1 What is a Mediterranean diet the secret to?

_____

[1 mark]

0 7 . 2 According to experts, what is the best thing about this diet?

_____

[1 mark]

0 7 . 3 Why is it surprising that Spanish people are still the biggest consumers of fresh fish and meat in Europe?

_____

[1 mark]

0 7 . 4 What further increases the benefits of a Mediterranean diet?

_____

[1 mark]

0 8 **Traffic in Barcelona**

You read this article in a Spanish online magazine.

Answers the questions in **English**.

> **Centro sin humos**
>
> Hace tres años cuando empezó la nueva ley de tráfico en Madrid mucha gente pensó que no habría ni beneficios económicos ni medioambientales. La realidad fue diferente: después de tres meses, el aire en las calles más céntricas de la capital presentaba un 55% menos de toxinas. Hoy en día, la Unión Europea admira a la capital española por estas medidas que benefician a la población.
>
> Así pues, la alcaldesa de Barcelona quiere que la capital catalana tenga el poder de decidir su propia política de tráfico. A partir del próximo noviembre, las restricciones en la segunda ciudad más poblada de España podrían ser mucho mayores: la alcaldesa quiere reducir drásticamente el número de coches los días laborales.

0 8 . 1 What did people expect to happen after the introduction of the traffic ban in Madrid?

_____

[1 mark]

0 8 . 2 According to the article, how soon after the implementation of the traffic ban did the air in central Madrid show a 55% reduction in toxins?

A	three years
B	three months
C	the following November

[1 mark]

0 8 . 3 What is the mayor of Barcelona asking for?

_____

[1 mark]

0 8 . 4 What specific change does the mayor want to see?

_____

[1 mark]

| 0 | 9 | **Bagless supermarkets**

You read this article in a Spanish newspaper.

Moncho y el medio ambiente

Moncho es un joven español apasionado del medio ambiente.

Es famoso en su barrio porque tiene tantas ideas para proteger el medio ambiente. El año pasado, a Moncho le preocupaban la falta de agua en España y, sobre todo, la deforestación del Amazonas. Este año, dice que los residuos plásticos amenazan nuestro planeta y perjudican seriamente la salud de los sistemas acuáticos.

En este momento sus esfuerzos se concentran en las bolsas de plástico de los supermercados. A Moncho le encantaría que el gobierno español fuese más radical, como el gobierno de Nueva Zelanda que acaba de prohibir su uso. Además, afirma que es mejor ir a los supermercados con nuestros botes o bolsas reusables y no comprar más bolsas nuevas, porque podemos ahorrar un poco de dinero y, además, contribuir a reducir la cantidad de plástico.

Actualmente, España es el quinto mayor productor de plásticos de la UE. Además, se calcula que el 35% de los peces de agua salada han comido plástico. Según Moncho, no cabe duda de que esta estadística es una vergüenza para la humanidad y hay que actuar ahora.

Write the correct letter in the box.

| 0 | 9 | . | 1 | What was Moncho **most** worried about last year?

A	The lack of water in Spain.
B	Deforestation in the Amazon.
C	Plastic waste.

[1 mark]

| 0 | 9 | . | 2 | Why does Moncho want Spain to be more like New Zealand?

A	New Zealand's government has just banned the use of plastic bags.
B	New Zealand's supermarkets now charge customers for plastic bag use.
C	New Zealand has radically reduced its use of plastic more than any other country.

[1 mark]

| 0 | 9 | . | 3 | According to Moncho, how should we feel about the statistics relating to plastic use?

A	Angry.
B	Shocked.
C	Embarrassed.

[1 mark]

Section B   Questions and answers in **Spanish**

| 1 | 0 |

Opiniones sobre la Tomatina de Buñol

¿Cuál es la opinión de cada persona sobre la Tomatina de Buñol?

Mario	La inmensa mancha roja de la Tomatina es alucinante. Es una tradición que hay que disfrutar juntos.
Clara	Parece una festividad sin cultura. ¿Asistiré yo? En honor a la verdad, es muy poco probable.
Rosa	Hay gente que dice que es violenta pero los tomates están maduros. Me hace gracia ver las fotos de la gente cubierta de rojo.
Pablo	Lo bueno es que no parece arriesgado asistir, aunque para mí hay mucha gente y está demasiado concurrida.

Escribe

P si la opinión es **positiva**.

N si la opinión es **negativa**.

P+N si la opinión es **positiva** y **negativa**.

| 1 | 0 | . | 1 | Mario   [1 mark]

| 1 | 0 | . | 2 | Clara   [1 mark]

| 1 | 0 | . | 3 | Rosa   [1 mark]

| 1 | 0 | . | 4 | Pablo   [1 mark]

1 | 1   **Las asignaturas más complicadas**

Lee este artículo sobre las asignaturas de secundaria en los institutos de Nicaragua.

> Nicoleta Puertollano, directora del centro educativo María Pineda, siempre pensó que las asignaturas más difíciles eran las científicas, la biología o la química, por ejemplo. Pero después de los últimos exámenes finales su opinión cambió radicalmente: los idiomas son lo más complejo.
>
> En su instituto se estudia latín, francés y alemán y este año han suspendido casi la mitad de los estudiantes. Al leer los resultados, Nicoleta estaba muy sorprendida, pero a partir de este año va a poner una solución a este problema: cada estudiante de idiomas tendrá una hora extra con un asistente extranjero y nativo.
>
> El problema es que nadie es hablante nativo de latín, pero Nicoleta tiene la solución: los estudiantes podrán leer unos divertidos comics en latín para practicar esta lengua.

Contesta a las preguntas en **español**.

1 | 1 . 1   ¿Cuándo cambió Nicoleta su opinión sobre cuáles eran las asignaturas más difíciles?

_____

[1 mark]

1 | 1 . 2   ¿Cómo reaccionó Nicoleta cuando leyó los resultados de los estudiantes de idiomas?

_____

[1 mark]

1 | 1 . 3   ¿Por qué no habrá un asistente de latín en el instituto?

_____

[1 mark]

1 | 1 . 4   ¿Qué podrán hacer los estudiantes de latín para practicar más?

_____

[1 mark]

1 2 **La sociedad y el medio ambiente**

Lees en un blog estas opiniones sobre los problemas sociales y medioambientales.

> En mi barrio, me preocupa mucho la falta de contenedores para reciclar botellas de plástico y vidrio. Menos mal que en mi instituto los estudiantes y los profesores reciclan latas y cartón.
>
> **Hasim**

> Me alegra saber que el pueblo recicla todo el papel semanalmente. Además, hay tiendas de ropa de segunda mano que intentan ayudar a los sin techo. Mi madre trabaja en una tienda de segunda mano los viernes.
>
> **Pamela**

Contesta a las preguntas en **español**.

Ejemplo ¿De qué se preocupa Hasim?

<u>La falta de contenedores para reciclar botellas de plástico y vidrio.</u>

1 2 . 1 ¿Cómo ayuda al medio ambiente el instituto de Hasim?

_____

[1 mark]

1 2 . 2 ¿Por qué está alegre Pamela?

_____

[1 mark]

1 2 . 3 ¿Qué hace la madre de Pamela para ayudar a los sin techo?

_____

[1 mark]

1 3 Padres e hijos: las relaciones

Ves esta página en una revista sobre las relaciones familiares. Tres expertos dan su opinión.

Experto A	Lo que sugiero firmemente es comer juntos; compartir una comida deliciosa es la excusa perfecta para hablar sobre temas problemáticos.
Experto B	Los adolescentes siempre evitan hablar con sus padres sobre el instituto o sus amigos. Por eso, recomiendo a los padres que siempre hablen con sus hijos mientras hacen las tareas del hogar. A veces, cocinar juntos el fin de semana es una buena situación para hablar.
Experto C	Un problema muy común es cuando los hijos quieren salir con amigos y volver tarde por la noche. ¿Cuál es la hora ideal para volver? Depende de las circunstancias, pero los padres deberían dialogar y decidir sobre los horarios con sus hijos.

¿Cuál de los expertos expresa cada opinión?

Escribe la letra correcta en la casilla.

1 3 . 1 Es una buena idea compartir los quehaceres. [1 mark]

1 3 . 2 Es recomendable almorzar en familia. [1 mark]

1 3 . 3 Puedes preparar algo rico con tu hijo. [1 mark]

1 3 . 4 Hay que tomar una decisión juntos sobre cuando regresar a casa. [1 mark]

1 4 En el camping

Completa el texto usando las palabras de la lista.

Escribe la letra correcta en cada casilla.

El Camping Las Nieves en Ruidera es estupendo. Allí se puede _____ la tienda de campaña cerca del lago y los ríos, donde también es posible _____ en sus aguas limpias siempre con atención de recoger todo al final del día para no _____ el ecosistema.

[3 marks]

A	subir
B	bañarse
C	buscar
D	montar
E	limpiar
F	dañar

1 4 . 1 ☐

1 4 . 2 ☐

1 4 . 3 ☐

Section C   Translation into **English**

| 1 | 5 |

Your Peruvian exchange partner sends you this article.

Translate it into **English** for a friend.

> ¿No te gusta la radio local? ¿Detestas las telenovelas predecibles? ¡No te preocupes! Ahora puedes elegir entre más de cien canales con nuestro nuevo sistema audiovisual. Con una conexión a Internet rápida, podrías escuchar la radio o ver películas de cualquier parte del mundo. ¡Para registrarte con nosotros, simplemente completa el siguiente formulario!

[9 marks]

_____

_____

_____

_____

_____

_____

_____

_____

_____

_____

END OF QUESTIONS

Answers and mark schemes

AQA GCSE Spanish (9–1)

PRACTICE PAPER

H

Higher Tier Paper 4 Writing

Time allowed: 1 hour 15 minutes

Instructions

- You must answer **three** questions.
- You must answer **either** Question 1.1 **or** Question 1.2. Do not answer both of these questions.
- You must answer **either** Question 2.1 **or** Question 2.2. Do not answer both of these questions.
- You must answer Question 3.
- Answer **all** questions in **Spanish**.
- Answer the questions in the spaces provided.
- Cross through any work you do not want to be marked.

Information

- The marks for the questions are shown in brackets.
- The maximum mark for this paper is 60.
- You must **not** use a dictionary during this test.
- In order to score the highest marks for Question 1.1/Question 1.2, you must write something about each bullet point. You must use a variety of vocabulary and structures and include your opinions.
- In order to score the highest marks for Question 2.1/Question 2.2, you must write something about both bullet points. You must use a variety of vocabulary and structures and include your opinions and reasons.

Please note: The Practice Paper questions and answers have not been written or approved by AQA.

Answer **either** Question 1.1 **or** Question 1.2.
You must **not** answer **both** of these questions.

EITHER Question 1.1

| 0 | 1 | . | 1 | Tu amiga colombiana te manda un email sobre su familia.

Respóndele y menciona:

- qué cosas hiciste con tu familia la semana pasada
- con quién te llevas mejor en casa
- si prefieres pasar el fin de semana con tus padres o con tus amigos
- cómo vas a celebrar el cumpleaños de un miembro de tu familia.

Escribe aproximadamente **90** palabras en **español**. Responde a todos los aspectos de la pregunta.

[16 marks]

OR Question 1.2

| 0 | 1 | . | 2 | Tu amigo cubano quiere saber qué deportes y actividades haces en tu tiempo libre.

Escríbele un email.

Menciona:

- qué deportes y actividades hiciste el verano pasado
- tu opinión sobre los deportes acuáticos
- qué haces en educación física en el instituto
- qué otras actividades te gustaría hacer en el futuro.

Escribe aproximadamente **90** palabras en **español**. Responde a todos los aspectos de la pregunta.

[16 marks]

_____

_____

_____

_____

_____

Answer **either** Question 2.1 **or** Question 2.2.
You must **not** answer **both** of these questions.

EITHER Question 2.1

| 0 | 2 | . | 1 |

En una visita a Málaga en España, ves un anuncio sobre cómo proteger el medio ambiente.

> ¡CUIDA TU CIUDAD! En Málaga, puedes…
>
> - Usar nuestra red de transporte público
> - Reciclar plástico y vidrio en más de 200 puntos
> - Llevar tu ropa usada a puntos de recogida

Decides mandar un email al ayuntamiento de la ciudad. Menciona:

- qué hiciste en Málaga para cuidar del medio ambiente

- tus recomendaciones para mejorar el medio ambiente en la ciudad.

Escribe aproximadamente **150** palabras en **español**. Responde a los dos aspectos de la pregunta.

[32 marks]

OR Question 2.2

| 0 | 2 | . | 2 |

Tu vloguero español favorito pide a sus admiradores que le manden emails con el título 'Por un mundo mejor´.

> **Vloguero Miguel**
> ¡Un mundo mejor es posible!
> ¿Te preocupa la pobreza? ¿El paro, el medio ambiente o el consumo de drogas?
> ¿Tienes buenas ideas para ayudar?

Decides mandar un email.

Menciona:

- qué problemas has visto en tu área recientemente
- qué harías para solucionar estos problemas.

Escribe aproximadamente **150** palabras en **español**. Responde a los dos aspectos de la pregunta.

[32 marks]

0 3 Translate the following passage into **Spanish**.

> My sister is going to get married next July and my parents want to buy a house. My father works in the town centre and yesterday we visited a big flat near to his office. It does not have a garden, but I would like to live there because I need my own bedroom.

[12 marks]

_____

_____

_____

_____

_____

_____

_____

_____

_____

_____

_____

_____

_____

END OF QUESTIONS

Model answers and mark schemes

AQA GCSE Spanish Higher Practice Papers © Oxford University Press 2020. Photocopying prohibited

OXFORD
UNIVERSITY PRESS

Great Clarendon Street, Oxford, OX2 6DP, United Kingdom

Oxford University Press is a department of the University of Oxford.

It furthers the University's objective of excellence in research, scholarship, and education by publishing worldwide. Oxford is a registered trade mark of Oxford University Press in the UK and in certain other countries

© Oxford University Press

British Library Cataloguing in Publication Data
Data available

978-1-38-200704-7

10 9 8 7 6 5 4 3 2 1

Paper used in the production of this book is a natural, recyclable product made from wood grown in sustainable forests. The manufacturing process conforms to the environmental regulations of the country of origin.

Printed in Great Britain by Ashford Colour Press Ltd, Gosport.

Acknowledgements
Cover illustrations: vectoriart/iStockphoto

The publisher and authors would like to thank the following for permission to use photographs and other copyright material:

Photos: p21: fizkes/Shutterstock; **p22:** BlueOrange Studio/Shutterstock; **p23:** Monkey Business Images/Shutterstock; **p69:** SpeedKingz/ Shutterstock; **p70:** Pressmaster/Shutterstock; **p71:** Friends Stock/ Shutterstock; **p119:** Halfpoint/Shutterstock; **p120:** wavebreakmedia/ Shutterstock; **p121:** Christian Martinez/Dreamstime.

Although we have made every effort to trace and contact all copyright holders before publication this has not been possible in all cases. If notified, the publisher will rectify any errors or omissions at the earliest opportunity.

Links to third party websites are provided by Oxford in good faith and for information only. Oxford disclaims any responsibility for the materials contained in any third party website referenced in this work.